Look Good in a Suit:
A Guide to Entering the Legal Profession

By Brian Radcliffe

Copyright © 2017 by Brian Radcliffe Publishing LLC

No part of this publication may be reproduced, distributed, or transmitted in any form or by any means, including photocopying, recording, or other electronic or mechanical methods, without the prior written permission of the publisher, except in the case of brief quotations embodied in reviews and certain other non-commercial uses permitted by copyright law.

Table of Contents

Introduction 5

PART 1: Pre-Law School Preparation 9

    Chapter 1: High School 11

    Chapter 2: College 22

    Chapter 3: On the Precipice: Between College and Law School 29

    Chapter 4: Decision Time 50

PART 2: Law School 85

    Chapter 5: First Year 87

    Chapter 6: First Summer 106

    Chapter 7: Getting a Job 124

    Chapter 8: Second/Third Year 147

PART 3: Successfully Entering the Legal Profession 163

    Chapter 9: Types of Practice Areas 165

    Chapter 10: Types of Legal Employers 179

    Chapter 11: Law Firm Taxidermy 188

    Chapter 12: Inside a Modern Law Firm 203

    Chapter 13: Succeeding as a Summer Associate 219

    Chapter 14: Surviving and ~~Thriving~~ Surviving in the Lions' Den: Making it as an Associate 230

Introduction

Rumor has it that you are interested in becoming a lawyer. Lawyers must be comfortable with ambiguity and multiple ways of looking at an issue. Here are two ways of looking at your interest.

First: Run! The legal profession requires years of extra school taking away both years of the best part of your life as well as hundreds of thousands of dollars in cost. Gaining employment of any kind in the legal profession is extraordinarily competitive, and remaining in a legal job long-term even more so. For those interested in the private sector, while the promise of high salaries in exchange for those years of hard work sounds nice in theory, in reality, such salaries are only available to a small percentage of lawyers and the financial rewards are potentially much smaller than what you could make in the financial or business world. Even if you "make it" as a law firm partner or top corporate lawyer, you will in all reasonable likelihood have endured years of round-the-clock client and partner demands that dramatically change the way you view your personal life and may involve lost relationships and even marriages. Your own personality may change as you face the harsh treatment of supervisors. Those with an idealistic streak and interested in public service may be similarly shocked by how difficult it is to obtain plum public service jobs as well as the lack of idealism and high level of naked competition in such environments, exacerbated by the significant difficulty in lifestyle that the low salaries provided by such positions entail. After a few years, you may, parallel to your for-profit lawyer colleagues, wonder whether your idealistic goals could have been better served in a non-legal capacity.

If you are still reading this book after that initiation, I have another reaction to you: Check you out! Even without making a single step beyond your initial interest in the legal profession, your very interest indicates that you likely have many positive personal qualities that will serve you right in life, whether in the legal profession or another one. You may have, or are working on, excellent communication skills such as speaking or writing in an articulate and clear fashion. You may have an interest in the business world, our political system, and/or the fundamental legal rights that make our society unique both in the world as well as in human history. You are clearly ambitious, hardworking or willing to be, and may have strong beliefs in doing what's right, whether it's for your client or for a larger public goal. You are considering a profession with long-term stability and a significant floor on demand, in which many enjoy relatively high salaries and a challenging professional life providing interaction with smart colleagues. No matter how long you last in the legal profession, the development of skills necessary to become or thrive as a lawyer will also be immensely useful in many other endeavors (as well as simply being a searching person and informed citizen), and lawyers frequently go on to succeed in the highest echelons of business and politics.

The truth is, these reactions are not contradictory. There is perhaps no profession that carries with it as much baggage, positive and negative, as the legal profession. It has been that way for a long time. "The first thing we do," Dick the Butcher said in Shakespeare's Henry VI, "let's kill all the lawyers."[1] Lawyers, or even the very raising of the prospect of lawyers, raises negative feelings in many people and brings to mind painful disputes, personal or professional problems, and mind-numbing minutiae. However, for many, the law alternatively or also brings to mind associations with high intelligence and educational success, public service, power, prestige, and upper middle-class respect. 800 years ago, Western civilization changed forever when the King of England accepted the Magna Carta that declared that the rule of law reigned supreme even over him. Every day, lawyers change the world, and they will continue to do so for the foreseeable future, as long as it is the law that holds ultimate power over our society.

In writing this book, I am not trying to reconcile these two competing narratives. Further, I am not going to attempt to convince you to or to not go to law school or enter the legal profession. Moreover, this is not a test

---

[1] Part II, act IV, Scene II, Line 73.

prep guide and I will, aside from a few tips, not be giving you the secret tips you need to ace the LSAT, law school exams, or the Bar. What this book gives you is a comprehensive, frank, and practical guide to what is involved in entering the legal profession, without spin, exaggeration, or bias resulting from personal incentives. I wrote this book because I found that the many perspectives existing regarding the process of entering the profession, whether a pre-law advisor in college or career counselor in law school, a jaded lawyer who feels that their career is not sufficiently successful, or employed lawyers, focus on their own successes or failures or their own interests, exaggerating the problems of a profession from which many derive financial and professional fulfillment, or refuse to be frank and specific about what one needs to succeed in the profession.

This book will proceed chronologically along your journey into the legal profession. It will start with high school and the initial preparatory work and thinking you may involve yourself in at that point, as well as a discussion regarding whether the college admission process is important to your success in entering the legal profession. Next, I will discuss skills to develop during one's college years and provide a framework for analysis on whether to, after college, apply to law school, analyzing both whether to work before applying and whether to apply at all. The next step is the application process, and this book provides many tips and tricks for use in the LSAT and law school applications, as well as a discussion on judging which law school to attend if one receives multiple offers.

After one enters law school, the first year looms, as the first year of law school is more important than in any other graduate school. In addition to academic and extracurricular success, the book provides an extended treatment to the all-important subject of how to obtain employment both during the summer after one's first year as well as a "summer associate" at a law firm after one's second year. The book then discusses strategies for approaching one's second and third years of law school. While this book is not meant as a bar review guide, it provides a short discussion on strategies to use while studying for the Bar.

Next, perhaps the most important topic of the book - how to obtain and succeed at an entry-level attorney position. The book provides a taxidermy of the legal profession, breaking down both types of legal employers as well as potential long-term career paths within the legal industry. It provides tips and tricks for succeeding first at a summer associate position. Finally, it provides a frank discussion of how to cope with and even succeed at a law firm while maintaining one's well-being and best interests.

So read carefully, hopefully enjoy, but above all, please don't highlight. That's so lawyerly!

PART 1
Pre-Law School Preparation

Chapter 1: High School

I. Developing Raw Skills

As we will see later, the law is particularly noteworthy for its acceptance and almost celebration of a wide variety of scholastic and developmental backgrounds. Thus, while schooling or reading subjects related to the law, or high school work experience in related fields are useful simply to add to your knowledge, there is no need to think about preparing for a legal career in any substantive way during high school.

However, the legal profession does place considerable value in and stress on certain fundamental skills and competencies. This is true at every stage in one's career - on the LSAT entrance exam, throughout law school, and in legal work itself, regardless of practice area. To be sure, factors such as hard work, raw intelligence, and a wide variety of other factors are also extremely important to success. However, skills matter, and a basic level of skill, no matter how cynical one is, is a prerequisite for success in any part of the legal world.

As a result, it follows that the more one becomes proficient and interested in these areas, the more likely one is to succeed at all of these stages. In turn, it makes sense to give yourself sufficient time to develop these skills along the eighteen years before college rather than cram all of that work into the four years or so of college. Therefore, this chapter analyzes the types of skills one can look to achieve even before college, although it's never too late to start.

What skills are we talking about, and how can one develop these skills, strategically with a view towards the law or simply for their use in life in general?

a. Communication Skills

The first skill set relevant to legal practice is communication, both written and oral. Developing your skills in this area is at once the most basic, most important, and most transferable legal skill to any avenue, professional or otherwise of life. You need communication skills to make and keep friends, to influence people, and to succeed in a workplace of any kind, so it should be no surprise that they are also important to a legal life.

Both written and oral communication skills are central to one's success as a lawyer because all important legal work involves written or oral communication. When I define the category "important work," I mean work by which your performance will be directly judged and on which your advancement will be based.

In this category, there is first the obvious work you may do for public consumption. What is involved in this type of work depends on your practice area. As a litigation attorney, trial advocacy, of course, revolves around persuasive oral communication, but given the current state of decreasing trials, it may more likely be the difference between a brilliantly or sloppily written summary judgment motion or pretrial hearing argument that determines your client's fate. For other types of legal work, the end work product is a contract or agreement, and again precisely worded contractual provisions may mean the difference between a successful outcome and an ambiguous provision ripe for the counterparty to refuse to obey.

But even outside of such obvious final outputs, there will be many other checkpoints where such skills will be crucial. How you communicate with clients, supervisors, adversaries, and counterparties is, perhaps, even more crucially important to your career than such final work. In these communications, you will be required to translate dense complex material into succinct and clear, yet precise formulations that reach the outcome you are seeking. With a client, it may be to explain the options before him or her, or steer them into choosing one particular option. With adversaries and counterparties, you will need to both strongly represent your clients' interest while maintaining a positive relationship with such parties to potentially reach an agreement. With supervisors and colleagues, you will need to communicate a willingness to serve as a team player while carefully advancing your personal interests.

Perhaps the best reason to hone your communication skills *ad nauseam* is that, whether or not you work on them, many of the other lawyers you work with in these capacities will have extraordinary abilities in this area, and you will be endlessly compared to them. Ah, now you're interested!

How to refine your skills in this area? Simple: Write and speak as much as possible. Taking writing courses is a start, but also consider writing for the school newspaper and finding outlets for creative writing, even poetry. Truly persuasive writing is elegant and even at times beautiful. You can also work on your oral communication skills prior to college. Engage in debate, work in student government or other student groups inside or outside of school, participate in meetings, and take leadership roles, where you will need to use communication skills to organize people and achieve success. You can also look to engage with the real non-student government in various ways, such as advocacy and internships. Find jobs that develop your written and/or oral communication skills rather than working another summer as a lifeguard.

b. Argumentation

The second critical skill is argumentation, or more precisely, learning to differentiate between slight variances in preferred outcomes of a particular issue and how to advocate for one side or the other. Success on the LSAT and law school is directly tied to this skill, and success in legal work is also tied to it. This skill is useful in other fields as well - an entire section of the GRE is devoted to logical reasoning and argumentation and asks for an argumentative essay quite similar to that asked by professors in law school exams.

Perfecting your skills in distinguishing between different positions is not just for future trial attorneys and litigators. Attorneys advising clients on transactions and regulatory matters also must distinguish between slight differences in contractual language or transactional structure and be able to persuasively advocate for their client's position, asking for one type of language or the other. You also may need to interpret complex statutes and statements from governmental bodies in advising your clients on how to proceed without running afoul of regulations, which is a large and growing area of practice.

How do you develop your skills in this area? You do not need to engage in formal disputation such as in debate societies to learn these skills. You simply need to develop a passion for issues. A simple way is to simply follow the op-ed pages of a newspaper such as the Wall Street Journal or New York Times. Read the arguments and see how the better essays explain the issue, marshal facts and evidence, and analyze the material in a cogent manner leading to a conclusion in favor of their position. Better yet, read both conservative and liberal opinions on the same issue and see how they each carefully and selectively choose the best facts supporting their opinion and analyze them in a supportive fashion.

c. Diligence

Legal practice of any kind will require you to engage in tedious, complex, detail-oriented work. You will need to be able to sit at a desk for 5, 10, 15, or even 20 hours at a time drafting, editing or reviewing legal documents. Sometimes, lawyers must pull multiple all-nighters in a row or go with only a couple of hours per night of sleep for weeks at a time. Many lawyers waste years gaining admittance to and attending law school and securing employment, only to learn belatedly that they do not enjoy being a lawyer. They may even despise it. This lack of interest results in an inability to find a niche or other area of expertise. The careers of such individuals frequently flounder.

It is inadvisable to go into such a serious, expensive, and time-consuming career without having some interest in it and in particular in the detail-oriented nature of the work involved. Although there are other avenues to use a law degree outside the law, many times the people seeking such opportunities could have secured such careers without incurring $200,000 in debt, losing income for three years, and having to explain why they are interested in a career change.

What can you do to assess or increase your diligence in consideration of a legal career? The below chart provides some guidance regarding this question. It may be unclear why some of these statements are important for a legal career; I will attempt to explain each of them at one point or another during this book.

However, no diagnosis is perfect in this regard. Speak to yourself frankly about this issue as well. For example, while you may not enjoy such tasks, think about whether you'll be willing to do so in certain circumstances (such as, for instance, if you were paid a significant amount of money!).

Can you ... Do you ... Will you ...

Do you have significant trouble with sitting and focusing for hours at a time on complex, relatively uninteresting tasks?

Are you comfortable working for long stretches of time by yourself, or would you be unhappy unless social interaction is a ubiquitous aspect of your responsibilities?

Can you see yourself pulling all-nighters? How about multiple all-nighters in a row? How about a month where you sleep no more than 3 hours per night?

Can you remain professional, happy, and perky even when working under the above conditions? How about if your boss is boorish, demanding, and facially unappreciative?

Are you motivated by clear finished products, or are you able to feel accomplished through more ambiguous work along with generalized professional and financial success?

Do you need to be in a starring role in projects or can you serve in a supporting role?

Are you interested in complex documents and abstract legal concepts, or will you feel unfulfilled unless you focus on projects with a clear practical result?

Can you be an order taker? Maker? Both at the same time?

Can you work in a bureaucratic, large organization where your role is limited, and your standing is amorphous and indeterminate?

Can you work well with supervisors, colleagues, and subordinates with a wide variety of personalities, including those who are demanding, arrogant, snide, or condescending (or all of the above)?

Can you remain highly intellectual, productive, and professional when under physical and emotional stress for an extended period of time?

Can you read, understand, and be able to apply long complex texts or other documents?

Are you interested in business transactions? Most high-paying legal work will involve business transactions of some kind, whether in terms of documentation for a transaction or litigating the transaction after it blows up.

On the other hand, will you be unhappy if you are not actually engaging in business transactions, but rather only advising on certain aspects of them, if, when and to the extent requested, and without your client necessarily viewing you as business savvy or part of the team?

II. College Admission

As you should know, if you don't already, the most important purpose of a high school education in terms of professional preparation for someone looking to enter a field requiring higher education is to matriculate to college. Anything one learns in high school can also be learned in college and employers do not generally expect professional development to begin in high school.

Now, even the singular task of gaining admission to college is, of course, extraordinarily difficult and requires a significant amount of studying to keep one's grades up as well as engaging in extra-curricular activities to add to one's application. But does even that one important task of getting into college matter? Being admitted to top colleges, previously a merely feverish affair in the United States, has now become a horrific, gladiator-style battle, with students and their parents frequently assuming that such decisions may make or break a young man's or woman's entire life. For a legal life, is that true?

At least with regard to the law, I am here to tell you: no, it is not. What undergraduate institution you attend will have remarkably little impact on even obtaining your first job out of law school, let alone on your career generally. Let's compare two law students: Law student A is named Proletariat Patricia. Patricia is a 2L at an elite law school, perhaps top 5 or 10, but only has a bachelors' degree from a third tier college, such as a secondary state or city university. Law student B, Bourgeois Bob, attends a top 30 law school and has a bachelors' degree from the Ivy League. As a rule, Patricia has a much better chance of obtaining a job with a top law firm than Bob. If Pat is in top quarter of her class, and Bob is in the bottom half, Pat, assuming she does not display extraordinary anxiety at her interviews, becomes almost certain to obtain that brass ring of a job at some top firm, while Bob is almost certainly out of luck, unless he has extraordinarily good connections.

Those of you with familial, personal, professional and/or emotional connection to elite colleges are no doubt enraged at what I just wrote. To be clear, I am not implying that an Ivy League education has no marginal benefit to a lawyer above that of a public or other private school. Far from it. Such an education will no doubt serve one well both academically as well as in the connections, both gained while at school and throughout one's career, that one will gain from joining such an environment. Further, there are additional utilitarian reasons to get an elite college degree as well. First, while a bachelors' degree from an elite college is far outweighed in importance by a degree from an elite law school, all else being equal, certainly a more-elite bachelors' degree improves one's resume dramatically. That pedigree will last one's entire career. Careers are complex and for many involve switching in and out of legal work and among types of employers, and having a strong academic pedigree will serve one well in establishing high intelligence and standing. Even in terms of obtaining that first job, one does not know when one is matriculating to college how one will do on the LSAT or what law school one will be accepted to, and certainly, those with a stronger undergraduate pedigree will hold an advantage over their classmates at the same law school.

I am thus not making a recommendation that those with legal ambitions should not matriculate to the Ivy League if offered the opportunity. Of course, an Ivy League education is valuable to one's intellectual and cultural growth. In addition, an Ivy League education is invaluable and extraordinarily important to gain entry to and help one succeed in a variety of other occupations and professions in the event one decides not to enter the legal profession. Choosing to go to a non-elite college on the assumption of going to law school is, in some ways, a risk in that you are reducing the number of options you have, while going to an elite college will keep doors open to many other options with high returns.

However, I do believe it is important to reconsider matriculating to an elite college if two criteria are true: a.) you are dead-set on a legal career, and b.) you will be taking out significantly more student loans to finance an education at the elite college than you would if you attended a less prestigious university. This is because law schools are very expensive. Having a "double Harvard" on your resume rather than a single simply may not be worth an extra several hundred thousand in student debt. Currently, tuition at many law schools, not including living expenses, runs close to $60,000 per year. Schools provide little to no scholarships based on financial need across the board, and most elite schools provide little to no academic scholarships as well. Assuming you will be financing that cost with student loans, that is already a tremendous debt burden. If you add several hundred thousand of student loans from your undergraduate degree, even assuming that you obtain employment at an elite law firm and obtain upper middle-class income throughout your legal career, that is a crushing burden from which you may never escape, and may prevent or delay you from enjoying other aspects of life such as having children or eating food other than Ramen.

Ultimately, if your family is wealthy or is otherwise happy to underwrite your undergraduate education without relying on debt, then, by all means, Ivy up. But for those who need to rely on debt, you owe it to yourself to think twice.

III. Privilege

Related to the above discussion on elite college admission and debt, I want to discuss briefly the impact of "privilege" on a legal career. What I mean by this is: Does growing up in an wealthy or upper middle-class family help one achieve success in a legal career, and is the impact greater or lesser than the impact on one's chances in other professions? Growing up in a wealthy household likely may include attending private schools or well-regarded public schools, enjoying family friends that are themselves successful in professions such as law or finance, and participating in social activities that skew towards higher-income individuals.

My answer is that, similar to the discussion regarding an Ivy League education, such a background is certainly helpful to entering the legal profession, but not necessary. It would be impossible to deny that there are some advantages to an upper-class background, as upper-class culture is certainly a fundamental aspect of the legal and financial worlds.

The advantages of a privileged background in the legal profession are easy to understand. Having such a background may provide one with numerous connections in the elite legal and financial world; such connections will be endlessly helpful in business matters such as securing employment (both immediately after law school and throughout one's career) as well as landing clients. More directly and immediately, it will also help one relate to the many others from such backgrounds who populate these worlds. As has been documented thoroughly over the past few years, over the past few decades, the lifestyle of the upper class has diverged significantly from those of the middle and lower class families. As social scientists have pointed out, upper and middle-class families in the United States increasingly behave quite differently in a variety of ways - from leisure activities, such as sports and vacations, to language, political views, and even dress.

In some cases, a recruit may not be extended an offer for entry level employment at elite firms if he or she does not exhibit personal qualities identified with the upper class. Of course, no one will ever give this reason explicitly; instead, they will say that the recruit does not have a good "fit" with the culture of the firm, which can be interpreted as not having a team player personality. Indeed, those making such a decision based on such criteria may not even realize that they are doing so. By example, business is frequently conducted in the legal and financial worlds in high-end restaurants, many law firms take potential recruits out for a lunch in such a venue prior to making an offer and summer associates at large law firms are expected to attend lunches frequently in such restaurants with full-time associates. Some of those from lower class backgrounds may be uncomfortable in such environments; the experience of one such person is documented in the best-seller, Hillbilly Elegy.

However, advantages of pedigree are only on the margins. Candidates who fit the criteria of firms in terms of law school pedigree and grades and are able to carry on a basic conversation should be confident in their ability to obtain employment regardless of personal background. Moreover, there are always enough strong candidates that weaker candidates with familial connections are well advised to be loath to mention such connections during an interview; such connections are best used only to obtain interviews in the first place. For candidates with outstanding intellects, firms will extend offers anyway, and assuming that one does gain employment, one will ultimately have the ability to become comfortable with this environment.

Ultimately, while it behooves every law student to carefully examine whether they may have difficulties adjusting to the legal world, the impact of not having an upper-class upbringing is nothing you cannot overcome. It is well known that many children of immigrants, such as Martin Lipton, Joe Flom, and others, were not only extraordinarily successful in the legal field but made fundamental changes to their practice areas and in some ways fundamentally how law is practiced in this country. A significant percentage of successful lawyers grew up with a lower middle-class upbringing. Having a different upbringing is only one small obstacle to achieving success in the legal field - to be overcome, to be sure, with copious amounts of determination and hard work.

Chapter 2: College

Congratulations on entering college! I hear you're still interested in being a lawyer and hopefully, after starting to read this book, keeping a few other options warm as well. This chapter discusses how you can use your studies and experience in college to prepare for a legal career and ultimately make the decision whether or not to enter law school. It discusses strategies and approaches to college with a view towards a legal career, such as what major to select, what skills to develop and how to develop them, and also includes a discussion on summer jobs.

I. College Work

a. Preparing to Apply

If you are serious about applying to law school, you may be wondering how to best use your college years to develop your future application. Many high school students (and their parents) engage in a lot of activities with a primary or secondary motive being to enhance their college application. Whether this is misguided or not, whether colleges should reduce the weight they give to such non-academic activities or not, one comforting point in that law school applications place less weight than perhaps any other type of higher education program on extra-curricular activities, honors, and leadership roles. Law school applications are heavily weighted towards relatively objective criteria - LSAT scores and GPA. I believe that law schools use these two criteria for at least 50% of the determination on whether to admit, and at many schools probably closer to 60 or 70%. Law schools will refuse to admit it publicly. There are some exceptions, and indeed some schools may recently have increased their attention to "holistic" application factors, but those two factors are crucially important.

Thus, there is little independent needed to develop your application via participating in extracurricular and leadership activities. I use the phrase "independent need" because this does not mean that such accouterments do not help your application. Background and holistic factors are important to your application. However, the part of the application that law schools most value for bringing out these factors is your personal statement. If you don't explain your story in that essay, you should not count on admission officers affirmatively deducing it from your application. You need to hit these guys on the head in the precise spot they've requested - in the personal statement - with anything you want them to consider.

In addition, don't take this to mean you should not engage in such activities. Extra-curricular, non-profit, and other leadership opportunities may be immensely helpful in developing your social and leadership skills for use in your future career (and life). This is just a how-to on applying to law school, not a how-to on life.

b. Deciding on a Major

In the previous chapter I wrote that there was little reason to worry about substantive preparation for a legal career in high school. In another victory for slackers and procrastinators everywhere, that largely remains the case in college. This means that the decision on what to major in is essentially up to you; law schools, as a rule, do not use what you majored in even as a data point in deciding whether to admit or deny.

While there are practical benefits to learning certain subjects during college, these subjects are spread across various majors. Gaining a knowledge of business transactions if your college has a business school will help you gain credibility if you work in a corporate or tax-related practice area at a law firm or at a corporate employer. Gaining expertise in writing clearly and effectively, via a major in English or simply taking courses involving significant writing, will aid you in law school and throughout your legal career. Gaining an in-depth understanding of the political and legal structure of this country, via a major in political science or again simply taking coursework in the area, will buoy your ability to absorb material in this area during law school. However, as alluded to before, no one will check to see if you have completed coursework in any of these areas.

The strongest impact that selecting a major can have on a new legal career is on the narrative legal employers will expect you to provide concerning why you wanted to enter the legal profession generally and what specifically you want to do in the profession. A major may be a useful part of that story. But then again, you should be able to weave most majors, if you are thoughtful enough, into a cogent explanation and I would not advise you to let this factor, by itself, to cause you to select a particular major.

If anything, this analysis means that, all else being equal, you should select a relatively less competitive major in which you believe you will receive excellent grades. This is because law schools do use GPA as not just a data point but one of the most important criteria, along with LSAT score and personal statement, in deciding who to admit. Thus, deciding to select a major that is less difficult for you and therefore increases your GPA may help you get admitted to law school. You will receive little to no penalties for doing so, although there could theoretically be some majors at certain colleges that are known by admission offices to be extremely unchallenging.

In particular, while obtaining a business degree will improve your understanding of the business world and provide a credential, it is by no means essential. First of all, there are multiple alternative avenues if one is simply looking for a base of business knowledge. College students of all majors can select individual courses of interest in a business school and law students also have an opportunity in law school to take classes in corporate law and, at many schools, business classes via cross-registration at a university's business school. There are opportunities while working and through supplemental education to become familiar with business concepts.

A business degree is also only a marginal credential to most legal careers. Most and perhaps the vast majority of partners in the corporate departments of large law firms and general counsels of large corporations do not have an undergraduate business degree. Many of them did not even take business courses in law school and arrived at law firms with little knowledge of corporate law. Indeed, many lawyers look down at business degrees or are insecure given their own liberal arts backgrounds, so one would be advised not to overly promote the degree in a job search or work. Business people, on the other hand, typecast lawyers regardless of whether or not the lawyer in question also has a business background prior to becoming a lawyer. In addition, if one is interested in working as an investment banker or consultant at a top consulting firm for which a law degree may be insufficient, it is much more advantageous in obtaining such positions to obtain an M.B.A., perhaps in a joint JD-MBA program, than an undergraduate degree in business.

However, you should strongly consider majoring in the life sciences (biology, chemistry) or computer science if you decide to represent clients in the life sciences industry and/or practice intellectual property law, the hot legal field devoted to the protection of patents and trademarks. This field includes work in all of the typical legal areas such as high-stakes litigation, transactional documentation, and regulatory compliance, and also includes a niche field (one which has become less lucrative over time) involving filing for new patent applications. The subject matter in this field frequently involves highly technical and fact-based analyses of subject matter involving technology, life sciences, financial engineering, or other complex intellectual property matter. A degree in these areas will aid in your understanding of the subject matter and provide you with a significant credential. Indeed, many law firms or corporate employers will expect that young lawyers wanting to specialize in work relating to any of these subjects will have a degree in the subject; in some cases, they will expect an advanced degree. Ultimately, if you find these subjects interesting, it may be a good idea to select one of them as a major to provide you with an added advantage in this niche; certainly, it will not penalize you if you decide to not enter these niche fields.

Ultimately, a degree in business, computer science, or life sciences should not be undertaken as simply a utilitarian exercise. Rather, you should carefully assess what your interests are, what skills you want to gain, and how confident you are in your future goals. If one is at all unsure about whether to enter law school, one is well advised to consider obtaining a degree in a field that provides significant employment options outside of law school, although certainly at the most elite colleges one should likely have good options regardless of which major one selects. If one is certain to enter law school, one's options are somewhat broader.

c. Summer Job

Summer employment can be helpful to an aspiring law student in numerous ways. The first such benefit is gaining comfort with a serious work environment. It is critical to be comfortable in a high-pressured professional environment prior to beginning work as a summer associate at a law firm or other employer, as being comfortable in the environment is one way in which you will be assessed. While you may have already gained skills in this area in high school, you must be certain to do so in college. It might be particularly helpful to gain experience in a variety of work environments, perhaps, working in a startup one summer and a major corporation the next.

You can also benefit from the connections and experience you develop at these positions. If you work for or otherwise gain exposure to successful people during your college internship and enjoyed a good relationship with them, you should try to continue to keep in touch for years down the line. In addition, the experience adds to your substantive knowledge of the fields in which one is interested. Moreover, one can also use these positions to help build a credible "story" to use in one's personal statement on one's law school applications.

Third, and perhaps most importantly, one can use summer employment to build up one's experience and resume for an alternative career path in the event one decides not to enter law school. As alluded to before, one may very well realize, whether after receiving a lower score on the LSAT than expected or simply after realizing that one's interests and talents lie elsewhere, that one does not want to go to law school. One will be much better positioned to transition to another field if one has already obtained paid or unpaid employment in a non-legal field, as one can use that experience to gain full-time employment in that field.

It is due to this broadening of interests that summer work can provide that I recommend that, in at least some of your summers, and preferably all of them, you obtain employment in fields unrelated to the law and hopefully in a specific field or fields in which you also may want to enter after graduation. The reason is because there are significant benefits to getting experience in other fields while there is very little benefit to gaining experience in legal work. Law schools and legal employers do not generally give preference to those who have employment in law-related fields prior to entering law school. Although such employment may be marginally helpful in crafting a meaningful story on one's personal statement, there are other ways to formulate such a narrative, and hopefully one will have something more meaningful to write in a personal statement than inspiration one received as a paralegal in a law office. While working in a law office could help you understand the practical ramifications of legal practice, you can just as easily obtain that by networking and practicing as a lawyer, which is very different from the administrative or paralegal tasks one will perform prior to entering law school. Indeed, as you might guess, this same advice to avoid legal employment also applies if you choose to work between college and law school, as discussed below.

d. Pre-Law Advisory

While as outlined above there are several aspects of your college years that can be helpful in preparing for law school, the pre-law advisory service of your college may be disappointingly less helpful. Every, or almost every, university has a pre-law advisor. While you might think that the person serving in this role may be an invaluable resource in navigating the law school application process, unfortunately, this is frequently not true. Pre-law advisors are generally not former happy, successful lawyers; if they were, they probably wouldn't take a pre-law advisory job. Many may never have practiced as lawyers even if they have a J.D, while others may not have found success or fulfillment in their legal careers. Some are clearly bitter about their experiences. Others are simply incompetent or worse - providing students, under the guise of expertise, with poor advice that will hurt their chances of acceptance more than if the students simply went with their gut.

This occurs because a pre-law advisor works for the school, and not you. This reality expresses itself in that, for example, a pre-law advisor is concerned with the rates of acceptance of the school's students into law schools in general, and not particular schools. Thus, the advisor may convince you to consider applying to schools lower down the law school prestige totem pole, when you would otherwise apply for a few prestigious schools offering the potential for elite employment or, if not admitted to one of those schools, otherwise enter another industry. Pre-law advisors will also provide you with the veneer of working with you on your personal statement. However, the advisor is responsible for a lot of students, lacks an intense familiarity with your unique life story, and, frankly, likely has a relative lack of interest in your success. As a result, he or she will usually not be able to connect with you on a personal basis sufficient to help you develop a statement that is sharp and personal enough to grab the attention of an admissions committee. He or she may also encourage you to take a load of coursework stereotypically suited for pre-law students, regardless of the lack of other options such coursework will provide you.

Even if your advisor fits the above negative description, that doesn't make he or she a bad person. It just means that, like with all aspects of your life, be sure to look out for your own interests without assuming that others already do. I will affirmatively discuss strategies and approaches for your law school application later; for now, know that you must avail yourself of advice other than relying passively on the advice provided by your school's appointed advisor.

Chapter 3: On the Precipice: Between College and Law School

This chapter discusses whether and when to go to law school. This chapter first analyzes, even if one wants to go to law school, the benefit or detriment of taking time off between college and law school. Second, it analyzes the question of whether or not to go to law school.

I. Working Between College and Law School

As you wind down your college career, even if you are confident in your desire and chances of receiving offers to enter law school, you may wonder whether you should apply to enter law school the year after college graduation or wait to apply one or more years after graduating. As you may know, a large percentage of law students waited at least a year after college to apply.

You should carefully think about this decision. There is no clear right answer, but it is a serious issue with meaningful ramifications for your career, although no resulting irreversible problems.

The reason to enter law school immediately is clear: You start making high legal salaries earlier. Assuming that your law school education will pay off with a good job, and your earnings will only grow as your career progresses, waiting before entering law school is simply leaving money on the table. If you are planning to work full-time anyway, seemingly, there is no reason to leave money on the table and trade in a large six-figure salary for the mid-to-high five-figure salary you are likely to, in all but a couple of industries, receive as a recent college graduate.

Indeed, the mistake of waiting seems even more extreme if you assume that you are going to make partner a certain number of years after you graduate law school. Let's make that 10 years. Thus, if you graduated law school at 25, you make partner at 35. Many law firms require partners to retire at a certain age, frequently 70. With those assumptions, waiting to go to law school just decreased the number of years you could serve as a partner from 35 to 33. Essentially, by waiting you simply lost two years of the multi-million dollar paydays you make as a law firm partner. Looking at it that way, waiting to go to law school is downright dumb.

However, there are several reasons to wait. There are six reasons people frequently make the decision to work before entering law school - four good reasons and two bad reasons.

The first good reason is that working full-time will introduce you to a professional environment, with all of the politics, emotions, and hopefully collegiality that comes along with that. While hopefully by this point you will have gained a significant amount of professional experience from your internships, working full-time may provide you a very different experience, in particular, because you may have been treated with kid gloves at your internships. At a full-time job, you will be able to develop your professionalism, your communication skills, and your work ethic.

Such experience will be very helpful to you as a young lawyer. You will be assessed on your professionalism immediately upon entering a law firm. Of course, you may be able to develop such skills without working full-time between college and law school. You should honestly assess your own personal development when making this decision.

Another reason to wait is to develop substantive skills. This is extremely useful for some people, but a waste of time for others. There is a meaningful benefit to developing substantive skills for two groups. The first is if you are unsure whether you will obtain a high-paying legal job after graduating law school (i.e. everyone except students at the most elite law schools). Legal jobs are very competitive, and even good students may find themselves without a well-paying legal job after graduating law school. Those law graduates without experience in other fields frequently struggle to obtain positions in non-legal fields as many other industries view lawyers as overqualified.

Having substantive experience in another field will be very helpful in this situation.

The other group of people for whom pre-law substantive experience is useful is if you ultimately want to enter another field; perhaps, investment banking or consulting, either immediately after law school or after initially entering the law. Many lawyers look to transition in this way but those in other industries are frequently skeptical as to the qualifications of such individuals as well as to whether their interest is legitimate or just deriving from the fact that they don't like practicing law. Having years of substantive experience will help contextualize your interest and provide you with resume-building experience in the industry at issue.

A third good reason to wait is if you are unsure whether you want to enter law school. Working for a couple of years helps you develop as a professional, helps develop your exposure to and understanding of other lines of work, and simply provides you with the time to gain self-awareness before you make an expensive and significant decision such as entering law school.

A fourth good reason, perhaps, a great reason, is simply because you want to do something else before entering the horrible, no-good, boring world of working for "the man" as a lawyer. Perhaps, you may want to work somewhat less hard than you would as a lawyer to allow for a better lifestyle or travel. Perhaps, you want to try living in a new city or work in an interesting but less remunerative line of work, or obtain a graduate degree in a field with which you are fascinated. Once you become a lawyer, you will probably work very hard. You may not have the opportunities to engage in these activities until you retire, and by that time you may be dead, sick, or simply too boring to care any longer. Life is short, and you should treat it that way.

In addition to the four good reasons to waiting, there are also two bad reasons to do so. The first is working as a paralegal to gain exposure to the legal industry. As discussed earlier, paralegal work is frequently administrative in nature and will provide at best a very limited and incomplete introduction to the legal industry. Some paralegal work at some law firms is more complex, but it all depends on the law firm in question. The paralegals at the law firms I worked at frequently worked very long hours on tasks that were both mind-numbingly boring yet extremely important. Those with an intellectual bent may find themselves being screamed at for messing up on tasks for which they are overqualified and in which they are entirely uninterested.

Further, while you may gain exposure to the type of intense lifestyle and culture of law firms, again you should be able to get an understanding of this through networking and other mechanisms without having to lose years of your life. Here, instead of working as a paralegal, just read this sentence: Lawyers work very hard and law firm culture is frequently very physically and emotionally taxing. Got it? I just saved you two years of annoying paralegal work.

Another problem you will face if you work as a paralegal after college is that, in the event you decide to not enter law school, you will have lost out on the opportunity to work in industries other than law. The one saving grace here is that employers understand that paralegals working at the most elite firms are highly qualified and such paralegals will likely have meaningful exit opportunities to join other industries.

The second bad reason to wait is to gain an advantage in the law school application process. The vast majority of law schools, especially elite law schools, I believe, do not provide significant advantages to those who have worked before entering law school. One notable exception is Northwestern, which is well known for having a preference for older students, but for most, it's a wash. The best one can say in support of this rationale is that by delaying you do have additional time to prepare for the LSAT before taking it, and that may indeed improve your score. In addition, you could theoretically secure better recommendations from your supervisors at work, although asking for such a recommendation will raise the awkward point that you may be leaving the firm's employment relatively shortly, which, depending on the situation, could jeopardize your standing at the company or even your employment.

Again, this is an important decision. I encourage you to carefully weigh all of the above considerations and speak to people who may have considered the same issue. Ultimately, though, on this issue, I would advise you to go with what your gut tells you is right for you.

II. Impact of Choosing a Legal Career

The moment of truth has arrived: to go or not to go. I've downplayed the importance of many other pre-law issues in the previous chapters. However, there is nothing to be downplayed about deciding to go to law school. This is a decision that will affect the rest of your life and you should treat it accordingly.

How will it affect your life? It will change you in three ways - it will change you as a person, it will dramatically alter your financial situation, and, of course, it will impact your career. Each of these is discussed in turn.

a. Changing as a Person

First, entering law school will affect how others view you. There is a persistent, profound view held by many that legal practice is an exceptional field of employment. Lawyers are viewed as having some or all of a wide variety of personal, emotional, and professional traits. One of the most profound assumptions about lawyers is that they are narrowly focused. As a result of this, many lawyers find it difficult to be considered for other jobs, either because they were unable to begin legal employment after law school or simply out of a desire to transition, even though legal work involves many skills transferable to other lines of work. In addition, it has been almost universally accepted that law practice is more a combination of numerous niche practice areas, one of which each lawyer joins, than a unified profession, despite the universal skills each lawyer must possess to succeed and the substantial overlap in the subject matter.

Others of these stereotypes are even contradictions of each other. People think lawyers are hot-tempered, cold and boring, detail-oriented and careful, intellectual and thoughtful, aggressive, passive-aggressive, passive, hardworking, hard-charging, good writers, boisterous, and introverted. Some may view lawyers as business-savvy. Others, including many in the business world, view them as allergic to it and as a result, many lawyers find it difficult to transition out of legal practice to a business position. People view lawyers with disdain, respect, and admiration, sometimes at the same time.

Are any or all of these views actually true? Ultimately, as there are over a million attorneys in this country, each appellation above is, of course, true for some lawyers and not for others. Regardless of the truth, you must realize, particularly if you are not interested in legal practice long term, that others have such assumptions.

Becoming a lawyer may also affect your self-assessment in some way, potentially positive or negative. Many view simply being a lawyer as an accomplishment worth attaining even if it does not result in improved employment, and thus may be happier or more confident as a result of becoming a lawyer. On the other hand, many lawyers are more depressed and negative because they do not enjoy working as a lawyer.

Even scarier, many lawyers also change mentally, emotionally, socially, and physically in response to the pressure-cooker environment of law firms. Lawyers become ruder to their colleagues, family and friends, lose their temper and scream about minor issues, learn to backstab and speak snidely to denigrate others without looking bad, have little time to socialize, date or spend time with family, lose or (more frequently) gain weight, and have increased anxiety and depression.

Sounds horrible, right? There are two ways to assuage your concerns. First, statistics says that many of these experiences are only as a result of working in the particular environments of large law firms.[2] Lawyers at other firms

---

[2] http://onlinelibrary.wiley.com/doi/10.1111/j.1740-1461.2009.01150.x/full.

have much higher feelings of happiness and such "side effects" are much lower. Second, you also may change in many ways for the better from such an environment. You may become more professional, less sensitive, more confident and assertive, more diligent, less procrastinating, and more detail-oriented.

Becoming a lawyer may also affect how you behave. Many of my colleagues from legal practice and law school adopted stereotypical narrow-minded mentalities in terms of the ways they can contribute to a law firm or other employer. This reflects itself in young lawyers waiting for commands and sticking to the specific tasks they are assigned, practice areas becoming life sentences, and lawyers limiting themselves to the most linear exit opportunities and career opportunities. Others simply avoid creativity in their legal work, even when creative thinking in litigating or structuring a transaction is frequently what makes the difference for a client and distinguishes a lawyer from others.

Ultimately, the law will change you, and it is up to you and your values and strength of character to maximize the positive changes and avoid the worst of the negative.

b. Financial Considerations

It is obvious that becoming a lawyer affects your financial situation, including your net worth and your income. What is less obvious is whether this impact is positive or negative, and, perhaps intriguingly, that you might not know for a long time whether it was positive or negative. Below, I discuss whether and in what circumstances it makes sense to go to law school simply as a financial matter.

Your first financial consideration regarding law school is the massive mountain of debt you will incur if you do not have a family offering to finance your education or other means of paying for your degree in cash. At the time of writing this, the cost of tuition and fees at some law schools is approaching $60,000, so $180,000 for three years. The actual cost of attendance must also include room and board and other living expenses, and some law schools currently estimate that the total amount needed is approximately $90,000 per year or $270,000.[3] If you finance that entire figure, that is an extraordinary amount of debt to take on, especially at the very beginning of a working career.

Indeed, that amount is also misleadingly low because by attending law school you are giving up on significant earnings you could have made at a full-time job. Assuming you could have earned $55,000 per year, that is another $165,000 you have lost. Even assuming that you receive $40,000 from summer work at a law firm during law school, that brings the total figure of decrease in cash flow due to attending law school to an astounding $395,000.

Moreover, when analyzed in the perspective of what you will need to pay off those loans, the situation becomes, perhaps, even more dire for all but the highest earners. Assuming (a) you take out that $270,000 and even disregarding the interest that will accrue and become capitalized into the loan while you attend law school, (b) a 20-year payment period (among the longest available for private loans), and (c) a low 5.5% interest rate, you will be paying $1,857.30 per month, or $22,287.60 for those 20 years to pay that off. Assuming a 10-year payoff, that is $2,930.21 per month or $35,162.52. That is money you will have to pay off before spending a cent for housing, food or clothing, and from your post-tax earnings; assuming a 30% tax rate, you need to make $31,839.43 just to earn enough to pay your loans for the 20-year payoff and $50,232.17 for the ten-year payoff, again without spending a dollar on food or shelter.[4] Further, for those blessed with higher

---

[3] http://www.law.columbia.edu/admissions/graduate-legal-studies/tuition-fees-and-financial-aid.

[4] This analysis is assuming you pay off your entire debt. However, there are federal programs for avoiding how to pay off certain portions of student debt. See https://studentaid.ed.gov/sa/repay-loans/forgiveness-cancellation/public-service.

Also, some law schools have a program where the law school will pay off the debt if you work as a lawyer for a non-profit or governmental organization and make no more than a certain amount of money. These programs may make it possible for you to work as a lawyer, in addition in a position where you may make a meaningful difference in the world, without a crushing debt burden. However, keep in mind that these programs significantly limit the amount of money you can

earnings either from your own earnings or when combined with a spouse, the interest is not deductible from your taxes.[5] One final insult to injury is that having significant debt from college will make the hole you are digging by going to law school all the harder to emerge from.

In light of this dour introduction, is the debt ever worth it? You should analyze this question based on a realistic potential income opportunity from law, and not a dream of riches, and as compared to potential other careers available or potentially available to you.

i. The Partnership Mirage

Before assessing realistic income opportunities, one argument to immediately dismiss is that debt load is not relevant because of the extraordinarily high income that law firm partners receive, so that even if times are tough while an associate, it will be well worth it once one is elected to partnership. As discussed below, in reality, taking on debt to become a law firm partner is only a small step removed from buying lotto tickets on credit.

In the past couple of decades, major law firms have made it more and more difficult to become a partner. Law firms are run to ensure that profits per partner are as high as possible in the current year, and particularly higher than as many other law firms as possible. Moreover, after many years of implementing this, law firms have arrived at a strategic view that, in addition to not electing a significant amount of new partners, a law firm electing any new partners at all is no longer a guarantee; rather, it is an extraordinary business decision made only when clearly justified in light of specific needs, whether it is a need for client business already held by a partner, or a need for skills held by the partner in a practice area niche. In addition, at all but a handful of the most elite law firms in the country, being elected as a partner is not a long or even medium term commitment.

---

make. In addition, they are based on the total household income and not just the income from your own work. Thus, if you have a spouse with a significant income, they may not be available to you even if you do not.
[5] https://www.irs.gov/taxtopics/tc456.html.

Partners at most firms, even new ones, will quickly be expected to bring in new business or be asked to leave.

In turn, it is a very difficult task to bring in the type of clients that will be willing to pay the fees of a large law firm, a task that is made tougher because law firms also expect lawyers to bill a large amount of hours. At many law firms, lawyers are expected to bill 2,000 hours per year. This is 40 hours per week 50 weeks a year, not including business development work, continuing legal education, committees and law firm business, speaking to your significant other, friends and family, eating meals or using the restroom. (Except for those who unfortunately do bill for using the restroom.) When the only time you have for business development is a few hours on Sunday afternoon, how exactly are you supposed to bring in millions of dollars of business? A good question indeed.

The only exception to this rule is perhaps a handful of the most elite law firms, such as Cravath Swaine and Moore, Wachtell Lipton, Sullivan and Cromwell, Skadden Arps, and Paul Weiss, which maintain sufficient marquee clients, brand names, and astronomical average profits per partner figures; such assets allow these firms to let their new partners develop for perhaps a decade without an expectation of immediately bringing in new clients. But even at these firms, the time will come for partners to put up or get out. And while these firms generally do have a continuing tradition of electing partners from the associate ranks, making partner at these firms is even harder, perhaps, than the excruciating task making partner is at most firms - I estimate that, perhaps, only an average of 1% of incoming new associates at such firms will make partner.

Finally, new partners do not receive even close to the profits per partner number that law firms report. Firstly, the reported figure is just a theoretical average and not necessarily received by any actual partners. This is because most law firms award profits simply based on how much business is brought in by the partner, so even senior partners without business will receive low salaries assuming they manage to stay around. It is true that a very small handful of firms, particularly the elite firms mentioned above, still have some sort of system known as "lockstep," whereby partners share profits with each other at least partially on the basis of seniority, although even this handful still modifies it in part to reward those with books of business. Second, at all firms, even the elite, recently minted partners will receive barely more than what they made as a senior associate. Indeed, because the new partner is no longer an employee, he or she will have to pay his or her own Medicare deductions and provide a capital contribution to the partnership, and the ultimate year-end return is frequently less than what was received prior to becoming a partner.

To be clear, I don't in any way mean to imply that becoming a partner is not possible or not a goal worth pursuing. It is and for you, it may very well be; hundreds of partners are minted every year. It's just not something you should assume.

ii. Analysis Based on Realistic Income

If not, what are good reasons to take on the debt, as a purely financial matter? Obtaining income as a law firm associate when one would otherwise only receive a much smaller income may indeed make sense, at least as an initial matter. Many large law firms provide first-year associates with a $180,000 initial salary, not including bonus. The law firms increase these salaries, frequently on an automatic basis without regard to hours worked and performance, each year. Senior associates can earn a $300,000 base salary.

However, taking out debt sufficient to cover tuition of the exorbitant kind mentioned above only makes sense at a handful of the most elite law schools, roughly the top five to 10. This is because it is only at those law schools that you have a significant enough chance of receiving offers to join a major law firm that taking out the debt is a good investment.[6] At these law schools, a very large percentage of students that are interested in working for a large law firm in a major market and are able to remain

---

[6] Not surprisingly, those law schools all charge high tuition at the top of the market.

relatively comfortable and personable during interviews will receive at least one offer to join a summer program. In turn, the vast majority of participants in these summer programs generally receive full-time offers to join the firm they worked at.

iii. Comparison to Non-Law Options

By going to law school, you are giving up on what may be a very promising, fulfilling, and rewarding career. You may be in college studying towards a degree highly sought by employers, or a couple of years after college working in a field where you are receiving good compensation and have excellent prospects. Even if you don't like the work you are currently doing, you may have opportunities to move within your current company or to another one or to an adjacent industry.

Let's be clear: By going to law school, you are likely giving all of that up forever. And it may be a tragic mistake to do so. Graduates of law school are expected by the world to practice law; potential opportunities to join other fields such as investment banking, private equity or consulting are generally only available to graduates of elite law schools and even for them it is highly competitive. Other industries frequently refuse to hire law graduates on the basis that they are overqualified, even when the candidate insists that they would love the position. It is rare for companies to even hire back employees who worked there and were well-regarded prior to attending law school. Generally, only those (such as accounting firms) where legal knowledge is valued if not required will consider doing so. Thus, by going to law school, you may be giving up a good job with a five or even six-figure salary for three years as a broke student and constant calls from debt collectors forever thereafter. This isn't an exaggeration. There are tens of thousands of former law students who, in essence, have ruined their lives by going to law school.

In addition to losing the position or industry you were in prior to law school, even if you are successful, you also will lose a significant amount of financial freedom. Once you take on the debt necessary to graduate law school without support, you must work at a job providing a significant income just to pay off your debt and live even somewhat comfortably. Without debt, perhaps, you will be able to obey the urge you get a few years down the line to do work that is less lucrative but is more meaningful for you, or throw everything away and become a vagabond moving from hostel to hostel. With the burden of debt provided by the friendly folks at the student aid office of your local law school, while there are certain federal programs to help, it will be much harder to do so.

Even if you don't currently have a particularly fulfilling and/or remunerative job right now, there may be many other opportunities that await you in the next few years without the need of a law degree if you devote sufficient time, hard work, and diligence. After all, even if you get a good job after two years of searching, you've still come out way ahead of where you would be if you went to law school - three years of zero pay plus six figures of debt.

I emphasize this so starkly because the situation for many law school graduates is indeed grim. There is no formal check on how many graduates can enter the legal industry like the medical industry does by tying the number of seats in medical school to the number of residencies. Every year, even in the best of times, thousands of law school graduates, even those from relatively well-regarded schools, cannot find meaningfully acceptable full or even stable part-time work. Even the ones that do may only receive compensation for full-time work below $50,000 with poor benefits - not even enough to cover the debt, let alone living expenses. The ones that don't are forced to accept anything, including menial jobs reviewing documents and getting paid by the hour for as low as $20 per hour. Even those jobs are quickly being eliminated by computerized document review programs.

A final consideration: Even where it could make financial sense to attend law school based on a strong likelihood of success in obtaining fabulous entry-level employment as a lawyer, there are still several financial reasons to consider alternative career paths. Associates frequently last only a few years at law firms, either because they cannot take it anymore, due to performance, or simply due to lack of work or to allow room for new associates. Associate-level salaries are not an annuity and should not be treated as such. Given the lack of partnership possibilities, most associates ultimately look to work at smaller law firms or other employers such as corporations where, while the lifestyle may be better, the compensation may be less, at least initially.

In addition, while law firm associate work is attractive in some ways due to the relatively straightforward process of obtaining positions and the standardized compensation, there may be many other forms of work in which you can earn competitive compensation without a law degree. Various jobs in the financial/securities industry, high-tech and computer-related industries, and various jobs in the business world, among others, provide very competitive compensation. Even when initial compensation is lower, high performers can rise quickly, as structures are less formalized than the fixed associate classes in law firms. Better yet, you don't have to deal with lawyers all day, you don't have to be a lawyer, and no one even cares what you got on your LSAT.

If you are dead-set on being a lawyer in particular, then by all means law school it is, but if you are simply interested in making money, and especially if you are ultimately interested in a job outside the law, you may want to consider whether trying to achieve your ultimate goals without law school makes sense, at least initially. In other words, you may not know for a long time, or ever, whether it makes sense from a financial perspective to choose law school over other options. That's why in this next section I suggest you analyze non-financial considerations as well.

c. Career Considerations

In approaching this weighty topic (keep in mind, this is the rest of your life we're talking about), I urge you to think a bit philosophically: What do you want from life? From work? If only we could approach life in those aggressive terms. How about this: What would satisfy you? Think about what would satisfy you in terms of a career in three ways: actual tasks, potential advancement and opportunities for change, and the purported "security" provided by a law degree.

i. Tasks

The first thing to realize is that the work you will do as a lawyer, especially as a junior lawyer, will be relatively detail-oriented. This work will be extremely important to your supervisors, their clients, and absolutely cannot be screwed up. This is in direct tension with the attraction of many individuals to the law for the opportunity to perform interesting public-facing work whether advocating at a trial, or clinching a merger, or involvement with fascinating legal concepts such as constitutional law.

I am not here to say that such work is a fantasy. On a relative scale, at least, legal work is frequently less detail-oriented than other professions such as accounting or actuarial work. In addition, many lawyers do perform high-profile and/or highly interesting on a regular basis.

There are also areas of the law that are less detail-oriented, such as advisory practice where you advise financial institutions, healthcare companies or other highly regulated companies on complying with rules and regulations. While, even in such areas, you will need to be very careful to understand the complex regulations at issue, and you will have to deeply understand the specifics of the business issues in play, at least you will not be assessed based on issues such as typos in documents or incorrect citation sentences. Further, the more senior you advance, you will increasingly be able to delegate the more mundane detail-oriented tasks to junior attorneys.

However, you must keep in mind that the vast majority of the tasks you likely will do as a junior lawyer, and a significant portion of what you likely will do for your entire career, will be highly technical work such as research, carefully preparing legal documents, reviewing documents, and collecting facts. Thus, for example, if all you really want to do is write, legal work may not be for you, even in a litigation practice, as writing will only be a portion, at times even a minuscule portion, of what you do even in such a practice.

Another consideration is that most lawyers only work in supporting roles; if it kills you to not be in charge, law may not be for you. If you fantasize about starting a company or making big investments in existing companies, from a perch as a practicing lawyer you will only be able to gain a limited view assisting others in such quests. You will at best be drafting documentation, documenting corporate governance, and/or making the appropriate filings to paper the transactions and decisions that the business people have decided to engage in. Even in litigation, a more lawyer-centric activity, ultimately what you file or don't file depends exclusively on the decisions of your client. You may think that the litigation the client tells you to file is counter-productive and stupid, and you may even try to warn the client as such, but it is ultimately the client's decision, not yours, and you will have to carry out their decisions regardless of your own feelings (unless, that is, you want to lose all your clients). As a government lawyer, you may be working on high-profile matters, but at the end of the day you, too, will be advising your political clients as to the legality of whatever they are considering and mechanisms to achieve their goals, but not actually, for the most part, making the decisions on what goals to shoot for.

ii. Advancement and Opportunities

Of course, just because you are licensed as a lawyer doesn't mean you can't leave practicing law to function as a decision maker. If that is one's ultimate goal, is the law a springboard or restraint on achieving those goals?

Like many questions in this book, the answer is somewhere in the middle and depends. For many, a law degree and background is an excellent way to accelerate a goal of achieving senior-level positions. In most industries, with the exception of finance and consulting, with just a college degree even the most talented individuals will start off at a relatively low pay scale. Advancement in pay and responsibility is idiosyncratic depending on one's relationships with one's superiors, the company's financial success, and myriad other factors. The individual is significantly dependent, for his or her career growth, on what actual responsibilities he or she receives, and if the individual finds his or herself at a failing company, a collapsing industry, or with little meaningful responsibility on one's resume, growth in one's career can become difficult - i.e. a "dead-end job."

A law degree can help in three ways. First, if one is successful in obtaining legal employment, one may enjoy a high starting salary that also increases annually. This positions one for similarly high salaries in the event one looks to transition out of law, as it is easier to ask for a comparable salary to one previously received than a significant increase. Working as a lawyer also provides one with substantive experience in, depending on practice area and law firm, business transactions, regulatory matters, and /or private and governmental dispute resolution. Depending on the law firm, some of your matters may be extremely high-profile. One will gain substantive skills in written and oral communication, crafting documentation, understanding corporate affairs, and /or governmental relations. Those with a legal background are assumed to have skills in some or many of these areas above. Thus, many lawyers transition out of legal practice to work in a wide variety of senior-level positions in government, business, and non-profit organizations.

iii. Security

There is also some basis, although overblown, to the widely held view that a law degree provides "security" for one's career.

The first way that law can serve as a security blanket is shielding lawyers from the worst effects when things go wrong. While those with business backgrounds or degrees may fly faster and higher, if they are caught at a collapsing company or, even worse, are implicated or work at a firm that is implicated in a scandal, they may be universally shunned as radioactive and unhireable.

Although lawyers at failed or investigated companies will likely still find it more difficult than most to move on, lawyers frequently avoid such scrutiny. Why? There are two reasons; one cynical and one sympathetic. The cynical view emerges from the realization that, well, lawyers write the laws, and thus many regulatory programs are either explicitly designed to or informally guided to investigate business people but not their legal advisors. Lawyers frequently shield their communications from disclosure to regulators and other parties behind the attorney-client privilege. Many have complained about the lack of prosecution of high-level individuals employed at financial institutions during the financial crisis, but have not similarly complained about the lack of investigations of their lawyers, despite the fact that financial institutions don't breathe without legal review. And to their unsung credit, the regulators did expend significant effort to investigate such individuals,[7] while again, the lawyers were generally not even touched.[8]

The more sympathetic explanation, applicable to both scandals as well as bad business decisions, is simply that, as noted above, lawyers are mere advisors and do not and by definition cannot, except in rare circumstances, actually make the poor decisions involved in a scandal.

The second security blanket is protection from the effects of the difficulty some business people have in gaining new opportunities when they become too experienced and senior. Once someone has obtained an extremely senior position at a corporation or financial firm, they frequently find it difficult to obtain similar positions at peer firms because the peer firms are both not

---

[7] https://dealbook.nytimes.com/2013/09/08/inside-the-end-of-the-u-s-bid-to-punish-lehman-executives/?_r=0.

[8] My personal view is that there may be reason to consider more expansive investigation of legal advice with regard to such transactions. Based on my experience, it has become apparent to me that business people rely on lawyers, particularly outside counsel, to serve as a safe harbor in considering transactions, and the outside lawyers very rarely issues strong negative opinions on such transactions regardless of the regulatory authority. The lawyers involved carefully avoid putting advice in writing and keep it context-specific enough to avoid future blame. At the end of the day, almost every single enforcement action involved business people and transactions that were extensively advised by highly qualified outside counsel. And while the business people involved frequently lose their jobs, the companies involved may suffer significant financial penalties and the lawyers simply continue to bill bill bill. At some point, some lawyers are serving as enablers, and that is unfortunate for everyone involved – the business people who are blamed, the company and its shareholders who received advice that ultimately damaged them, and everyone who believes in fairly administered justice and transparent markets.

interested in adding another person at that level, do not have positions at that level, and, most importantly, do not want to bring them in at a lower level. Thus, many such individuals end up opening consulting practices or other independent firms.

Legal work, on the other hand, is a bit more fluid. Thus, it frequently occurs that senior lawyers, even those the top of a reporting chain such as partners at law firms or general counsels in government or corporations, frequently move to positions where they may report to a more senior lawyer. And, at the end of the day, these lawyers can always just practice law in a solo practice, and if senior enough should be able to find employment, at least temporarily, at a law firm. Similarly, many lawyers who transition to an in-house corporate or government role frequently move back to law firm life, either their old firm or another, with their credentials now burnished with in-house or governmental exposure.

However, it is important to understand that this security blanket, like many benefits of a law degree, only protects a select few, those with significant legal experience and/or elite credentials. If you do not go to an elite law school, and you do not obtain significant legal experience and contacts, you may find yourself either immediately after graduation or after a few years of practice with few to no employment options acceptable to you. As mentioned above, thousands of law school graduates find themselves with very poor prospects. While working as a solo practitioner is technically available, the reality is that working as a solo practitioner is crushingly competitive in all but the smallest rural markets, with little to no distinguishing one lawyer from the thousands of other available lawyers. Constant business development is essentially 100% of the job, with legal skill largely irrelevant, and even the business gained frequently provides very low rates. Online automation and other technology-based legal service providers, such as the various "Uber-like" lawyer referral services now available, will no doubt continue to drive the profit margins of such commoditized work even lower. And throughout it all, the debt bills will continue to arrive every month on schedule.

Even for those with relatively good credentials and positions, the security purportedly provided by a law degree can be quite ephemeral in bad market conditions. In the throes of the financial crisis, many lawyers found themselves pigeonholed in esoteric practice areas such as structured finance that had collapsed. Even though they were employed by well-known law firms, after being laid off, they were unable to obtain meaningful employment. Even when such markets rebounded, the law firms looked to refill their bullpen with new graduates and avoided the unemployed.

Conclusion

In sum, there is no objective answer to whether law is a good career. Like any good lawyer, I leave the ultimate decision up to you. Carefully consider your talents, both academically and otherwise, your interests, and your risk tolerance. Above all, I urge you not to just consider these questions once before attending law school, but to continually do so throughout your career. A legal career is not made on day one, but depends on careful tilling as it sprouts and flowers. The actual outcome of the questions analyzed in this chapter on your career prospects and your job security depends on you choosing an appropriate practice area, developing skills and contacts, avoiding collapsing companies, and myriad other factors unique to the situation. Regularly assess whether you are meeting your original goals, whether they have changed, what you want to accomplish next as a lawyer, and how you want to go about doing so. Such rigorous self-assessment will do more than any generalities laid out here in helping you achieve your ultimate goals.

Chapter 4: Decision Time

Ready to take the plunge and apply? This chapter is ready to guide you through each step of the process. First, it discusses the LSAT and provides a general strategic overview as well as certain tips and tricks to doing your best on the test. Second, it provides strategies for carefully preparing your application, including the all-important personal statement essay, and timing the submission. Finally, it analyzes how to decide where and whether to go if accepted to multiple schools.

I. LSAT

The LSAT is unlike any test you have taken before. Not so much in content, although you'll see plenty of weird, wacky, wild stuff on the LSAT like logic games that hopefully you have never seen before and afterward will never see again. No, the real difference between the LSAT and every other test you've ever taken is that it is more important than all of the other tests you've ever taken combined. The LSAT is more heavily weighted in the law school admission process by most schools than any other standardized admission test in any other academic program. I estimate that the LSAT (or the GRE, for those few schools that accept that test) forms up to 50% of the criteria for admission at many schools.

You also must do well. How well? Let's take a look at a couple representative law schools. First, take Hofstra University School of Law. The school is ranked 118th out of 142 by this year's edition of U.S. News' annual law school rankings, informally accepted as the barometer of law school prestige. The school's median LSAT score is 151,[9] which is about or very slightly below the 50th percentile for the test. Hofstra, while no doubt possessing a strong faculty, is clearly not an elite school. Large law firms are generally not interested in students from this institution and students will need to do very well at the school to be considered for any well-paying jobs.

---

[9] http://law.hofstra.edu/jdprogram/admissions/classprofile/

And yet you may need to clear fifty percent of the field of LSAT takers, which is stronger than the field of SAT takers given that only those with academic ambitions are taking the test, to have a strong chance of being admitted to even this school.

Going to even incrementally better law schools will require significantly higher LSAT scores. The Case Western Reserve University School of Law is ranked 62nd in the US News ranking - significantly higher than Hofstra, but still a school where competition is fierce for good jobs. Yet its median score is 159, which is around the 77th percentile.[10] Have your sights set on a school like Penn Law? Study hard - the median LSAT score is 169,[11] or the 97th percentile - better than 97 out of every 100 test-takers.

Another distinction of the LSAT from other tests is that it has no connection to the material that test-takers studied in school. Even the SAT, which is known to be less tied to school material than its rival college test, the ACT, requires knowledge of math and verbal skills that a strong majority of students only learn in high school. The LSAT, on the other hand, simply hones in on test-taker's fundamental logic and reading comprehension skills. That doesn't mean that your score is innate and can't be changed - by all means you can and should engage in focused study of the skills demanded by the test and try to significantly increase your score. But there is no temporal limitation on when that studying and test-taking should take place, nor, again, any direct connection to your studies in school.

This lack of connection to your studies leads to one elegant and powerful hack: Because you don't need to take the LSAT at any particular time, everyone considering law school should try out the LSAT as soon as possible after you realize you might want to attend law school. If you are interested in law school at the beginning of college, take some practice tests during your freshman year or even the summer before. Take a couple of weeks, buy

---

[10] http://law.case.edu/Admissions/Class-Profiles.
[11] https://www.law.upenn.edu/admissions/jd/entering-class-profile.php.

a study guide or two, and study the skills demanded by the test and methods for improving scores.

If you are wildly off from your target, you should develop a "Plan B" not involving law school. To be sure, you can and maybe even should continue to be interested in law school, work hard in school, and take the LSAT later after intensive test prep. At the same time, however, you should definitely also take steps such as (a) obtaining a degree in a major with stronger job prospects or with greater potential for alternative graduate study than the major you would have taken if law school was the only plan, (b) obtaining summer employment in other fields (even though per above you should be doing that anyway) and (c) simply psychologically accepting the fact that you may be wildly successful in a field other than law.

But, you say, don't many test-takers improve 10 or even 20 points after intensive study? Yes, some do, but many test-takers may only improve five points or less on their scaled LSAT score even after months of practice and thousands of dollars spent on test prep. By all means aim for the fences, but by taking the test early you have just been provided an opportunity to have four extra years to prepare for the event that you get a single on your LSAT prep instead of a home run.

In any event, your actual studying for the LSAT should take place no later than your junior year in college if you want to attend law school immediately after college. Even if you want to work, you might find that you have much more time to study during college or summer breaks than when working full-time. Therefore, I encourage you to consider taking the test before you graduate college. Similarly, it will give you a head-start on preparing for life other than law school in the event you do not do as well as you would like.

How to begin a study plan? Start with an assessment test, which should be available free from a test prep company. This should be similar to your previous score, although it may be lower given that you may have taken the previous test under conditions that were less test-like than the official assessment run by the test prep company. The assessment will guide you as to how much work you have to do. However, be prepared to buckle down and study hard for an extended period of time even if your score is high, as even a few extra points more could raise the level of school to which you are admitted.

Next, you will have to decide what materials and assistance you should avail yourself of to prepare. The main question in this regard will be whether or not you want to join a test prep program, and if so, which one.

My view is that such services are definitely useful, and more useful to those who enjoy studying with others and being taught orally. Many types of learners, particularly those that learn best from oral instruction, social interaction, and being able to ask questions, will benefit from a class atmosphere. Others may benefit simply by discipline imposed by the program's set schedule.

However, if you are the driven type that can simply take books, buckle down and study, there is no reason you should not be able to get most of all the substance a test prep company offers while studying independently. Even the best test prep companies essentially offer four tools - methods, practice problems, practice tests, and answers to students' questions. You will be able to get the first three from self-study. You can purchase, for a nominal fee per test, published copies of official versions of all previously administered tests from the company that administers the LSAT. If you purchase 30-35 tests, that will provide more than enough practice tests and problems. Some of the test prep companies also publish books containing all of the substance from their lessons. While you will not have someone to ask questions, if you only have a relatively small amount of questions you should be able to cover that in a few hours of private tutoring at a fraction of the price of a full test prep program.

If you choose to join a program, which should you choose? I am a big fan of Powerscore, and that is my top recommendation for either choosing a full program or simply purchasing their books for self-study. The

Powerscore program provides methods for breaking down problems in all three sections of the LSAT. In particular, their methods for attacking logic games are far and away the best in the industry. Powerscore requires instructors to have extraordinarily high scores, and extensively vets and trains them. They offer self-study material, which is available for less than $125 on Amazon and is high-quality and clear, and the group study courses are excellent for those who are interested.

To be sure, there are other great choices for test-prep. Blueprint and Testmasters are two shops that I am also happy to recommend. Both of these programs offer high-quality methods and smart and engaging instructors. Instructors from Blueprint and Testmasters also have achieved extraordinarily high scores, are closely vetted, and receive extended training. Receiving instruction from such teachers is perhaps worth the substantial investment that a test prep program entails.

However, it's not true that you "can't go wrong." With Kaplan or Princeton Review, you can go wrong in a big way. I believe these large corporate firms are deficient both in their methods as well as their instructors. I believe their methods take a lot of time both to learn as well as to implement in practice, and on a test where every second counts, that is a material liability. Further, these programs have lower requirements for what score a teacher must have attained, and I believe that to be a truly great teacher you must have mastered, and not just understood, the subject area. Finally, I believe their customer service is not as good as with the smaller companies noted above.

These two firms can get by despite all these problems due to their name recognition, but I know many people who are unhappy former Kaplan or Princeton Review students. These students were upset both because they were still in need of supplemental instruction after completing the course and also because they were out several thousand dollars. Don't make their mistake.

This is not the place to provide an extended treatment of the best strategies for acing the LSAT. However, please, find below a few general thoughts on preparing for "the Test":

1. Devote as much time as you can on your LSAT preparation, even if your scores on practice tests are relatively high. The LSAT is much more important than a grade received in any particular class. Even an extra point or two could mean getting into the school of your choice. Prioritize LSAT study. Doing better on an LSAT leads, fairly directly, to a simpler path to achieving success in the legal industry, whether financial success for those in the for-profit sector or obtaining plum positions for those interested in public service. Remember that when you are deep in the weeds of an obtuse logic game, or when you can't make a dinner date with friends.

2. Be sure to take plenty of full practice tests (from the official previous tests released by LSAC). You need to take these tests on a regular basis to properly assess your progress. Further, when you take a full test, be sure to take it under true test conditions, or at least a relatively close approximation to such conditions. In particular, keep careful time and promptly stop work when the buzzer goes off. Time is a critical sorting factor for LSAT test-takers - everyone could get a perfect score on the logic games section if they had unlimited time. That extra minute you take on a practice test will not be available on test day and may be inflating your practice test scores materially.

3. However, focus on your drilling and do not rely completely on full-length practice tests. Full practice tests are only necessary to, every two weeks or so, assess your current standing and progress. But the main goal of practicing on real LSAT problems is to improve, and the most focused way to do that is to focus on those areas where you need the greatest help, rather than an entire test every time.

4. Many people score up to a few points lower on test day than they were scoring on practice tests. This is probably due to the increased anxiety on test day along with the increased difficulty of true test conditions. Keep that in mind when assessing your progress.

5. At least 24 hours before the test, preferably 36 or even 48, make sure to stop studying completely. If you've studied like you should, further studying will not help, and can only hurt. The LSAT is not a test like the CPA or MCAT where you are required to memorize information. It tests the ability to quickly answer certain logic problems. Whatever level you haven't been able to conquer in months of studying, a couple of extra days will not do it. Further, breaking away from studying will prevent you from becoming overly anxious about the test. Everyone will have a little anxiety, but being overly anxious and thinking too much about the test will only prevent your mind from focusing clearly on the problems at hand on test day.

6. Try to pace yourself to be able to take the LSAT by June of the year you apply. This will provide you with a clear understanding of those schools you have a good chance of getting into. In addition, if you are able to send your application in September, it will provide schools with the ability to assess your full application early in the application cycle, which may increase your chances of getting in. Finally, taking it in June will allow you to have an opportunity to take the September test as well if you don't do as well as you'd like.

II. Application

Itching to hit "submit"? Relax! The application process is perhaps the most straightforward part of beginning a legal career, aside from setting up direct deposit once the checks start rolling in. In addition, applying to law school is much more straightforward than applying to college and other graduate programs. This is because so many law schools have substantially identical required application packages.

I break up my thoughts on the application process into a corny division of "Who," "What," "Where," and "When." Specifically, I address whether you should seek help on the application from others with expertise, provide an extended analysis of attacking the pieces of the application itself, how to time your applications, and where to apply and accept.

A. Who - Getting Help

One question you may have is whether you should process your application yourself, perhaps advised by a pre-law advisor, or seek outside help from a paid admissions consultant. In the past few decades, dozens of admissions consulting firms have proliferated, offering potential college or graduate school students the potential to receive expert advice on preparing their applications. The best of these services are staffed with employees or consultants who previously served as university admissions staff in the educational level and field in question, or even served as head of admissions. These companies offer help with preparing an application generally, as well as targeted assistance with preparing a personal statement essay.

While this all sounds great, admissions consultants typically charge up to several thousand dollars for their work. Given the added cost, is it worth it?

My view is that if you locate a consultant that comes recommended, has good credentials, and appears to be able to offer some good advice, I would recommend you shell out the necessary cash. Applying to highly competitive programs is an idiosyncratic process, more so even than applying for jobs, and that's even though law school does not require the interviews and other annoying parts of applying to medical or business school. Law school admission committees are looking for, despite their protestations otherwise, certain themes in applications. Who is better than someone who actually sat at the other end of the table to help guide you to hit the hidden checkpoints?

In addition to this general value of providing value-added insight into what the committee is looking for, consultants will help you make your personal statement truly personal. As I will explain below, a personal statement must be poignant and real, inspiring and thoughtful. Everyone, yes, even you, has aspects of their life that can be used to create such a tapestry, but you may be so overly familiar with your own life that you are inured from identifying those aspects of it that would be noteworthy to others. Here, a consultant can step in, especially one armed with the sensitivity to what admissions committees find interesting.

B. What - Application Components

The below walks you through the different parts of that package and provides an extended discussion of the most important part - your personal statement.

Most law schools require that applications include five components:

- Answers to a series of questionnaire-like questions on personal and educational background, honors received, work experience, and extracurricular pursuits.
- Recommendations
- A personal statement essay, or a series of essays
- LSAT record
- Undergraduate transcript and any graduate transcripts

1. Questionnaire

The questionnaire portion is, as a general matter, fairly straightforward as it is factual. At this point, you have collected whatever honors and activities you have collected. Generally, all there is to do is fill it in. However, there are a few basic pointers to keep in mind:

a. Never lie. Don't even think about it. Don't even exaggerate. Don't even think about exaggerating. In addition to, you know, morality, it is a terrible idea because the consequences will be dire if you are caught. In any event (although this shouldn't be necessary to convince you), extracurricular activities don't matter much in the scheme of law school admissions, so it won't even help you dramatically to lie.

b. Don't create the impression that you believe that the work experience you have in the legal or business world or relevant coursework "qualifies" you for law school admission. As noted above, it doesn't, nor does lack of it disqualify you. In LSAT parlance, it is neither necessary nor sufficient. Indeed, it is not even that helpful. Law schools are careful to cultivate and protect their image as true academic institutions and not just professional schools. While your relevant experience may indeed be helpful in your future career, law schools are clear that they value a wide variety of backgrounds. I'm not saying to omit relevant information, especially since it may help form part of the basis for your narrative, expressed in your personal statement but also in your application as a whole, of why you are applying to law school. Just make sure to avoid arguing that the experience itself is sufficient of an explanation or qualifies you for admission.

c. Relatedly, given that law schools are interested in a pool of applicants that is diverse in every sense of the word, be sure to think broadly about what information is relevant for the questionnaire and in particular for a resume if submitted. Be sure to include interesting points about yourself, even hobbies or other interests, in an "additional information" section on the bottom of your resume. Draft the bullet points regarding the specifics of each position on your resume with an eye towards what you did in the position that is most relevant to you growing as a person and not necessarily the most directly relevant point to an employer. Think creatively about what you have accomplished, whether it be as part of a formal academic, work experience, or extracurricular activity, or informal life experience.

2. Recommendations

You can treat recommendations as a relatively low-priority part of your application process. Many law schools treat recommendations, unless they are truly unique, as relatively unimportant. To be sure, receiving an outstanding recommendation is certainly useful. However, by the time you are completing your application, the content of a recommendation is largely out of your hands – you cannot make someone have a high opinion of you. The most relevant advice for this portion of your application is to develop good relationships with your professors for when you will need them to advocate for you. While you may be able to submit recommendations from others such as work supervisors, typically at least one needs to come from a professor.

3. Essay

The personal statement is an extremely important part of your application in numerous ways. Your LSAT scores and GPA are objective numbers, and the personal statement is the way that you can explain subjectively why you as a holistic person deserve admission over other qualified candidates. While the application, in general, serves this purpose, admissions committees look to a personal statement in particular as the strongest vehicle to explaining the uniqueness of your candidacy. I believe many schools provide personal statements with up to 25% weight on whether to admit.

While a variety of academic programs look to holistic factors in an application and ask for personal statements as part of that inquiry, I believe that law schools are unique. Other programs, in particular, undergraduate programs, examine the application as a whole for such holistic factors and carefully review such points as extra-curricular activities and leadership positions. However, law schools hone in more narrowly on the personal statement.

The personal statement is also perhaps the area of your application over which you have the most control. LSAT and GPA and recommendations can be worked on, but are ultimately at least partially based on factors outside your control now. What comes out when you put pen to paper on your statement, on the other hand, is completely up to you.

As a result, I urge you to take the personal statement extremely seriously, about as seriously as you take the LSAT. Like with the LSAT, I urge you to start thinking about and drafting your statement as long before your application is due as possible. Like the LSAT, there is nothing inherently limiting you to the time period shortly before you apply to law school for such work. While you will continue to develop experiences potentially worthy for submission in the statement, you already likely have a significant amount of material long before.

Where to start? The best beginning to a personal statement is a comprehensive reckoning of you as a human being. What are your goals? What are you like as a person - what are the unique aspects of your personality? What are your accomplishments - personal, social, professional, and academic? What challenges have you overcome? And finally, which experiences in your life best illustrate your answers to these questions?

In performing this analysis, you need to calibrate your focus on those qualities which admissions committees value. As you may guess, an essay stating that you are a very competitive person who achieved academic success and now seeks financial and societal success as a highly respected corporate lawyer is not going to help your candidacy.

What are the types of qualities sought by admissions committees? Consultants should have lots of good thoughts here. However, in general, I believe that you might be able to summarize the qualities that committees are looking for as a.) strength of character, b.) interest in law, c.) interest in improving the world. You express these qualities in your essay through the experiences, goals, and views you share in the essay.

Is this code for saying that you want to save children in Africa? Many assume that law schools are looking for essays indicating experience and interest in liberal social justice causes generally, and in legal work on behalf of social justice-oriented non-profit organizations in particular. This suspicion is not baseless. Admittedly, it is impossible to deny that most law schools tilt liberal in both the average political affiliation of its faculty and staff as well as in the atmosphere created by the programs it sponsors, the official statements they make, and other aspects of the schools. In turn, staff members who work on admissions committees for a variety of academic programs are known to tilt liberal. A logical extension of the above is that the schools, consciously or subconsciously, provide preferences for students who are or at least claim or express interest in the same socio-political beliefs and causes as they do.

However, I believe this assessment is overly simplistic. I believe that law schools are at least consciously looking for the qualities outlined above. The basis for these criteria, however, is not a liberal social and political conscience but, as I mentioned above, an attempt to solidify the law school as a pure academic institution rather than a mere professional school. The objection that a committee would have to an essay simply laying out why one would be a good corporate lawyer is that it implies that the school is simply a vocational training ground for such work. Law school administrators, on the contrary, view their institutions as providing numerous benefits to the society, from serving as laboratories of policy, statutory and regulatory proposals, to providing unpaid legal services for underserved communities, to ensuring the rule of law is upheld. As you can figure out, many of these goals do overlap with goals of liberal political and non-profit groups.

What comes out is that by tethering your interest in law to the greater societal good and other aspects of yourself beyond your vocational goals, your thoughts may touch on themes also identified as liberal. However, what the law school is searching for is an indication that you fit with the law school's conception of itself as helping the greater societal good and not your affiliation with liberal orthodoxy per se.

In any event, when doing this analysis, I urge you to not leave any of your important prior life experiences unexamined when exploring topics to weave into your statement. Some of them you may view as irrelevant to law school; others simply uninteresting to others, and still others simply too painful to reconsider.

Please overcome any urges you have to ignore certain painful parts of your life; indeed, focus on those parts. Many times it is particularly the most painful parts of your life that have strengthened your character. On a practical (or cynical, if you view such uses as exploitative) level, admissions committees look to such experiences with interest. A good essay should be sufficiently personal and powerful to the extent that you would not necessarily be comfortable showing it to your friends, or even your family.

One final note on personal statements: Especially as I have championed the use of legitimate admissions consultants, I also feel a countervailing need to be clear that you absolutely should be writing your entire essay. Consultants are for consulting - for helping you figure out good ideas, for providing inspiration prior to drafting and feedback after. Anything more is abhorrent and wrong. Simply put, if you have someone write your essay, you are a cheat and a thief. You are a cheat because school places certain rules on how people are allowed to apply, in the same way that there are rules about how you take a test like a final or the LSAT, and violating those rules in order to gain admission is just as heinous as having someone else take your LSAT for you. You are a thief because you have stolen the admission from those who do follow the rules, and the knowledge that you have done so should, if you're not a sociopath, dog you for decades even if you do find success.

But forget about things like morals - it also might backfire badly. Admissions committees write passionately about how they are closely paying attention to any signs that applicants are submitting the work of others.[12]

You may argue that it is irrational for a school to base such a large criterion of its admission decision on an essay where there is little ability to determine true authorship and not expect rampant violation of the rules. Perhaps. But that is an argument for a general change in policy to focus more closely on objective criteria. That has no impact on the rules that are currently there, and apply to everyone, including you, equally.

---

[12] https://www.tuck.dartmouth.edu/mba/blog/so-you-want-to-work-with-an-admissions-consultant

Ultimately, only someone with a low sense of self-worth can even think that submitting someone else's story other than one's own is necessary for admission. Believe in yourself. You are a good person who has the qualities that admissions committees are looking for. Just dig deeper. (And, considering you just considered cheating, dig really deep indeed!)

C. Where - to Apply

1. Criteria to Distinguish Among Law Schools

There are three criteria that you should consider when distinguishing among law schools: prestige of the school, cost, and geographic considerations.

i. Prestige of the School

The more well-regarded the law school is, the more likely you are to receive offers for entry-level positions, and the greater ease you will have in getting other jobs in the future. This is true whatever field of law you are interested in. In turn, while it sounds crazy, the rankings by U.S. News do generally approximate how well-regarded a law school is, which makes sense since one of that publication's chief criteria for its rankings is a survey of professors as to the school's regard.

ii. Geography

Geography is important because the less prestigious a law school is, the more localized will be the entry-level employment opportunities provided by a degree from the school. While, like prestige, there is a continuum here, law schools can roughly be divided into two groups - "national schools," where a degree should offer you significant ability to obtain a job in most markets in the country, and "regional schools," where a degree generally only provides access to opportunities in the geographic region around the school. The "national" tier roughly includes the top 15 to 20 law schools, with all schools with lower rankings qualifying as regional schools, with the geographic limitations of the degree becoming more pronounced the lower the school's ranking.

If you decide to attend a regional school, you may very well be able to obtain jobs in other markets, either on an entry-level basis and certainly in the future. However, at least on an entry-level basis, based on percentages, it will be difficult to obtain such a position initially and you shouldn't assume otherwise any more than you would assume an annual 15% rate of return on your savings.

Geography is an important factor even within the subset of national schools. In recent years, more and more students who intend on practicing in a particular geographic area attend law schools outside of their geographic area, generally based on the view that the law school is more prestigious than those available in the geographic area and will provide a greater credential even within the geographic area. Law schools, in turn, have fervently recruited these students out of their desire to increase "geographic diversity."

While it would be a bad idea to go to a higher-ranked regional school outside of your geographic area, assuming you are dead-set on that geography, if you are able to get into national schools within your geographic area as well as more prestigious ones outside of the area, should you follow this trend and look to go to the most prestigious national school you can get into?

That is a very good question deserving a multilayered analysis. The first is the specific schools involved. If you are accepted to Yale or Harvard, it is hard to imagine a situation, barring an extraordinary scholarship offer, where you turn that down for geographic reasons. Other schools, such as, say, considering going to Penn instead of Northwestern or Texas, are a much closer call. The second point of analysis to consider is how serious you are about practicing in this geography, at least initially. If you spend three years at a school outside your geographic area, perhaps, one of the big East Coast schools, you may find yourself starting your career in the geographic area around that law school for various reasons, be they social (all your law school friends stayed), professional (the most prestigious firms are in the same area), personal (you met someone special), or psychological (you're a super lazy dude or gal and didn't want to take the effort to interview outside of the school's geography). Indeed, you may end up staying your entire life there. If you want to avoid this, for lack of a better word, temptation, you may want to stick to schools in your geographic area of interest.

The third question to consider is whether you intend on returning to your original area immediately after law school or only after a few years. If immediately, the law school is very prestigious, you do even relatively well, and you don't have weird practice area interests, it should not be all that difficult to obtain an offer to join a summer program where you want one.

However, if you intend on working for a few years before returning, then it may be more difficult to switch, as firms frequently hire numerous entry-level associates en masse while hiring lateral associates one by one, based on practice area needs. Each lateral opportunity will be different, you obviously may not get the first one you apply or interview for, and interviewing for 10 lateral associate opportunities is much more difficult if the interviews are a plane ride away as opposed to a subway ride away, especially since you likely have a very intense job to keep as an associate and are keeping your search private. While hopefully some firms will appreciate your scheduling issues, this situation becomes even more difficult if the firms request a second, third or even fourth round of interviews, as they frequently do. If you attempt to lateral to a new geographic area after several years of practice, you may find yourself looking for a lateral opening for several years or alternatively settling for a position that is less exciting than what you would have wanted.[13]

---

[13] However, this concern is somewhat muted if you decide to look for an in-house opportunity after working for a few years at a firm outside your area. If anything, there are many in-house opportunities in geographic areas outside the large geographic centers, as many companies look for cost reasons to locate in relatively

The final factor to consider is your practice area preferences. It is much more difficult to move from one geographic area to another as a litigation associate than a corporate associate, and it will also be more difficult to switch if you are in a niche practice area that is either not that important to the economy of the geography you want to switch to (think securitization or entertainment in Cleveland) or is simply small enough that there are not that many opportunities in that practice area in that geography to begin with. This is a factor militating in favor of either going to a law school in your preferred geographic area or alternatively obtaining a summer associate position in the area rather than working for a few years first outside of the area.

iii. Cost

Cost is an extremely important factor for most people in evaluating law schools. Indeed, it may be the only consideration. For most people who aren't going to law school to go into public service, law school is a way of improving their financial status. Essentially, then the entire inquiry is a comparison between the outlays in explicit monetary cost and opportunity cost of not working versus the financial rewards upon graduation and throughout a career. Indeed, even for those going into public service, this is still the same question you should be asking, assuming that you can get the public service job you are interested in from multiple schools.

First, you have to measure the cost of tuition. Here, there are two factors that make it less expensive to go to less prestigious schools. First, truly elite schools in the top 15 generally charge more than the regional schools. 11 of the 13 most expensive law schools are among the top 15 schools as measured by the U.S. News rankings.[14] Second, the lower prestige a school is, the more scholarship they are likely to provide an applicant who has gained admission to higher prestige schools. The first factor basically divides

---

inexpensive areas that may also be near production facilities, and if anything those opportunities may be less competitive for someone with the right credentials than the harsh competition for in-house opportunities in the big east coast urban hubs.
[14] https://www.ilrg.com/rankings/law/tuition/4/asc/Tuition.

law schools into two buckets - the crazy-high-tuition bucket of elite schools and the slightly-less-crazy-but-still-crazy-high-tuition bucket of regional schools. The second, factor, however, is a continuum going from Yale to the lowest ranked schools - generally, you will get greater scholarships the lower ranked the school is, assuming you qualify for higher schools.

2. Application to Actual Law Schools

There are nine "bands" of prestige within the top 200 law schools ranked by U.S. News & World Report, and the schools within each of which are relatively homogenous in terms of prestige.

i. Yale

Yes, a category of one. Yale stands alone due to its extremely small class size, lack of grades, and uniquely rigorous admission standards. If you go to Yale, you are essentially guaranteed an entry-level job at an elite large law firm should you desire one, and in addition, you will be automatically considered for a range of other positions in government and industry.

Yale graduates have a particularly helpful "leg up" on the extraordinarily difficult competition on getting a job teaching at a law school as a professor. These jobs were always competitive, and they have become all the more so given the well-publicized difficulties that many law schools and their graduates have had in recent years and the resulting laying off of faculty and even closing down of schools. Given that Yale is regarded, and regards itself, as a training ground for academic scholars, law schools as employers respect a Yale degree considerably more than any other.

If you are admitted to Yale, congratulations!

ii. Harvard

Being admitted to Harvard is an accomplishment that you will be able to impress people with for the rest of your life. It will certainly provide you with immediate opportunities to join a wide variety of elite law firms as well as other employers such as financial firms and consulting firms.

There are two distinctions between Yale and Harvard. First, Yale uniquely provides a cleaner path to the uber-competitive field of legal academia. In addition, the opportunities at elite law firms while plentiful will be less automatic than at Yale.

Understanding why that second point is true requires an explanation of how large law firms recruit at elite law schools. In addition to the uniquely high LSAT scores of the Yale student body, Yale has a small class size as it is - generally around 150 students - and many of these students are interested in working in academia or the public sector. This makes the pool of Yale students interested in working for large law firms significantly less than at any other elite law school. Generally, elite law firms look to retain relationships with all elite law schools and secure a minimum of a few students from each top school per year. The problem for law firms is, of course, that not every student to whom a firm extends an offer accepts the offer. Given how few students there are at Yale, and how coveted they are, law firms need to court essentially every member of the class in order to get a few students.

By contrast, Harvard is actually one of the largest law schools in the country, at approximately 550 students per class. Certainly, each of those students is bright, but at a class size that large, employers must only offer employment to a percentage of applicants to maintain relationships with other elite schools.

Despite the distinction from Yale, the Harvard cache will certainly grab the attention of recruiters and leaders at each stage in your career, whether you're looking to transition to a different firm, in-house, to public sector work or outside of law. You only need to look at the composition of the Supreme Court to understand - of the nine justices on the court before the death of Antonin Scalia, eight out of nine had attended either Yale or Harvard, with five, a full majority, from Harvard alone.

iii. Stanford / Columbia / Chicago / NYU

These schools are all hyper-elite. They require GPAs and LSAT scores roughly equivalent to those required by Harvard. A large percentage of the class at each of these schools comes from Ivy League or Ivy League equivalent undergraduate programs and the faculty of these schools uniformly consists of leading scholars in their fields.

Practically, matriculating to any of these schools will provide you a unique "leg up" both in terms of gaining an entry-level job as well as throughout your entire career. Landing in the top quarter of your class at any of these schools will qualify you to work at even elite firms, while landing in the top half will qualify you to work at basically any other firm. However, the reality is that this advantage is more by way of being practically helpful, that you will not be blocked from any employer because your law school is deemed insufficiently credentialed. At the end of the day though, you will still need to work hard to ultimately get anywhere or move to different jobs or fields. This is opposed to Harvard and Yale, which provide a true conversation-stealing way to impress and open doors.

In terms of gaining an entry-level job, the most elite New York City law firms will essentially guarantee a certain amount of offers to students from Columbia and NYU, with the same equivalence for Los Angeles firms and Stanford and Chicago firms for U Chicago. Many elite New York law firms will hire upwards of 100 summer associates each year, and will do everything in their power to make sure they have at least 15 or more from each of these schools, with less for Chicago given that it is a smaller school and sends more students to Chicago firms. Indeed, many elite New York law firms aim to and successfully do recruit more than 50% of their incoming summer associates from Yale, Harvard, Columbia, NYU, and either Stanford or Chicago, and they are very careful about maintaining good relationships with each of these schools.

However, a few caveats to the breathless excitement expressed by the last few paragraphs. First, it is no longer the case, like was true before the financial crisis, that every student at these schools is essentially guaranteed a job at a large law firm. While hiring has recovered since the lows immediately after the crisis, hiring has not recovered to pre-crisis levels, given advances in outsourcing and automation and lack of growth in the demand for legal services. As a result, if you do poorly on exams, you can still get a job at a large law firm, but you will definitely need to impress at interviews. The bottom quarter of these schools may find it difficult to obtain a position at any large law firm.

Second, NYU, while it is viewed as equivalent to the other Chicago and Columbia by elite law firms, is not viewed as quite the equivalent by federal judges, especially justices at the Supreme Court, in terms of selecting federal law clerks. While its standing has improved in recent years, it is only ranked seventh in terms of number of clerks it has sent to SCOTUS since 2000, which is more noteworthy considering that it has much larger class sizes than Yale, Stanford, Columbia, and Chicago.[15]

Third, prospective students should appreciate the trade-offs inherent in attending one of these schools and in following the most well-trod path after graduating them of working at a large New York law firm. As alluded to before, one of the top reasons that so many students flock to Columbia and NYU, in addition to the excellent legal education, is that those law firms hire so many students from these law schools. Many of these law firms hire upwards of 100 summer associates per year, so there are simply a lot of entry-level jobs to be had. However, as discuss in greater detail later, these law firms don't expand their associate count by 100 or even close to that number every year, which means that these firms expect very significant associate attrition. While mid-size and regional law firms also have significant attrition, at such firms there is still some sense that partnership is still a natural possibility if you are highly respected and work hard, while large law firms require a separate excuse for making every additional partner, and simply being highly respected is not enough.

---

[15] http://www.bcgsearch.com/article/900047770/Law-Schools-That-Send-the-Most-Attorneys-to-United-States-Supreme-Court-Clerkships/

Working at a New York law firm, and especially at the more elite ones, is thus, for the vast majority of associates, a temp job. By going down this path, as opposed to going to a regional school and working at a smaller firm, there is a more immediate need to devote time to your career development and thinking about what exit and career development options you want to create for yourself. There will hopefully be many options available to you, as many employers crave recruiting associates at big New York law firms, but these options are most available to those that carefully craft their development as an associate.

iv. Penn / Michigan / Virginia / Duke / Berkeley / Northwestern

This is the lowest tier that is still considered elite, the law school equivalent of the Ivy League. These schools all require high LSAT scores and GPAs and elite law firms heavily recruit at each of them. By this level, however, the level of relationship between each elite firm and the school will depend on specifics, with some firms recruiting more heavily at Penn and Michigan than Northwestern or Duke, and vice versa. Another school-specific quirk is that Supreme Court justices are known to have a sweet spot for Virginia students, with that school sending more than all but three other schools (Harvard, Yale, and Stanford) to such positions since 2010 and all but four other schools since 2000,[16] and an aversion to Penn, with that school ranking 13th since 2010 and 15th since 2000.

With a degree from such a school, employers will believe that you are bright and academically successful and that perception will certainly help you both initially and throughout your career. However, at these schools, you do need to study hard, and those at the bottom of the class will struggle to obtain employment at a large law firm, particularly if the student also has specific geographic or practice area criteria.

---

[16] http://www.bcgsearch.com/article/900047770/Law-Schools-That-Send-the-Most-Attorneys-to-United-States-Supreme-Court-Clerkships/

v. Cornell / Texas / Georgetown

These are the final schools that are legitimately considered "national" law schools in that law firms across the country will appreciate the degree. After this point, schools are generally "regional" schools which have excellent reputations and whose students are highly sought in the geographic area around the school, but the students of which will struggle to obtain offers at law firms in other areas. Already at these three schools, it will be significantly easier for Cornell students to obtain offers in New York, Texas in the South, and Georgetown in DC. However, this is still a matter of degree - there are thousands of Georgetown grads working as attorneys in NYC. It will just become harder the poorer one does in class rank.

vi. University of California–Los Angeles / Vanderbilt University / Washington University in St. Louis / University of Southern California (Gould) / University of Iowa / University of Notre Dame / Emory University / Boston University / University of Minnesota / Arizona State University (O'Connor)

This is the top rung of "regional" schools. These schools are very highly respected in the geographic area around them, where firms will look to actively recruit from them. By geographic area, I mean including the nearest big market, not just a ten-mile radius; thus Notre Dame is highly respected in the Chicago and Indianapolis markets. To be sure, they are also respected as good schools on a national level, and in major markets such as in New York, but the reality is that firms in other areas need to maintain their closest relationships with schools in their own area. As a result, if you do very well at one of these law schools, you will have a good shot at employment at a large but not elite firm outside of the school's geographic area, but little to no chance if you are in the bottom half of the class, unless you have unique connections or other very unique attributes to your candidacy.

Practically, this means that if you decide to attend one of these schools, you should be comfortable working short-to-medium term in the geographic area that hires most seriously from the school in question. This is especially true if you are taking out debt to finance all or most of your education at one of these schools and therefore need to work at a large law firm to pay off the debt. You very well may get that plum job you ultimately want in New York, LA or Chicago if you end up doing very well in the fierce competition of law school, but you should not take out $200,000-$300,000 on the assumption that you will outperform a hundred or two hundred other law students who are just as ambitious, hard-working and bright as you.

vii. <u>Schools Ranked 26-50 by U.S. News & World Report</u>

Law firms generally consider law schools in this band as second-choice institutions at which to recruit even if the school is in the same geographic area as the firm. The schools in this band that are located in smaller markets are highly prized by law firms in those markets, but in turn, there are simply less legal jobs available in those markets overall, so it will not be a straightforward exercise to obtain employment.

While it is hard to overly generalize, as a general matter, if you go to these schools you will need to do well to get a job at a mid-size or large law firm even in the market nearest to the law school in question. To have a good chance, you will generally need to finish the first year at least in the top half of your class, with your chances increasing significantly if you finish in the top quarter. If you finish in the top ten percent, you will have your pick of jobs. This is generally true even in competitive markets such as New York, where candidates in the top ten percent at Fordham have a relatively easy opportunity to get jobs at even the most elite NYC law firms.

On the other hand, if you finish in the bottom half of the class, you will likely have a small set of entry-level opportunities available to you. While employers do understand that schools in this band only admit students who have significant academic achievement, and if you work hard, network, and aggressively explore options you should be able to obtain legal employment, you will likely have to compromise on the type of practice area and /or the type and size of employer. However, the opportunities that will be present for these students may not be meaningfully better than those available to students in lower-tier schools.

viii. <u>Schools Ranked 51-100 by U.S. News & World Report</u>

By this point, you might be feeling offended that I am grouping a band as large as 50 law schools together. However, the reality is that, while each of these schools has a unique culture and set of academic opportunities, they are broadly similar in terms of the employment opportunities they offer. Law schools within this band located in major metropolitan centers are generally considered third choice for firms seeking entry-level attorneys. You will need to do well, perhaps very well, to obtain entry-level employment as a lawyer at a salary level that will permit you to pay off significant debt. While, again, it is difficult to generalize, this means that you need to finish within the top quarter of your class to obtain employment at a mid-size or large law firm. If you do very well, such as in the top 10% of your class, Law Review, or similar, you will still have opportunities to obtain employment similar to those available to students at the top 15 law schools, except that you will be limited to those firms in the primary geographic legal market around the law school.

If my tone sounds foreboding, it is intentional. While it is true that thousands of graduates of these schools build fine careers, with many of them working at the most prestigious law firms, corporations, and financial institutions in the country, there are also thousands, indeed tens of thousands, of students from these schools that will never get close to this ladder of success. A large percentage of students at such schools - certainly the bottom half and many in the top half - struggle to obtain any full-time employment as an attorney, regardless of salary, practice area, type of work, or type of employer. For those that do, many will not even earn enough to pay back their loans, and certainly not also have a comfortable middle-class lifestyle, let alone the upper middle-class lifestyle stereotypically held by lawyers and the wealthy one held by successful ones.

There are few options available to the many graduates of these schools who are unable to gain entry-level employment. The option of opening up one's own law firm is, of course, always technically available, but, given that it is also available to the hundreds of thousands of other lawyers in the country, it is excruciatingly difficult to make ends meet when opening up your own firm without first obtaining connections and experience through prior work experience. While state and local government and some federal agencies will hire such students, such jobs are also extraordinarily competitive, generally easier to obtain by those with prior experience, and the salary will be small at least at first. The decision to go to law school has led many of these students, barring further career reinvention, to a life of constant running from collection agencies.

On the other hand, it certainly is true that students at these schools still have the opportunity to obtain the exciting entry-level opportunities provided by more elite schools, and perhaps while saving tens of thousands of dollars due to academic scholarships. One caveat is that, even if you are fortunate to obtain lucrative entry-level opportunities, the lack of name recognition of the school on your resume may impact your career if you look to make a lateral move to another firm or in-house. A federal or state supreme court clerkship, if you are fortunate to obtain one, may help alleviate this problem and further bolster your credentials. At the end of the day, if you work hard and carefully develop your career, once you get an elite law firm on your resume, most employers will appreciate your credentials and aptitude, and that will become even more so as your career advances.

ix. Schools ranked 101-200 by U.S. News & World Report

Schools at this level are a third or fourth choice for employers even within the markets they primarily serve. At most schools within the first hundred law schools, employers will actively recruit students by going on campus to interview students and marketing themselves to students to make them interested in applying for positions. Of course, the extent that they do so depends on where the school ranks within the band - at the top schools, students will be able to obtain on-campus interviews with the firms they are interested in most without regard to how well they are doing academically, and all of the elite firms will throw cocktail receptions for students so that they can meet current partners and associates. At those schools lower in this band, only students with certain grades may be permitted to obtain on-campus interviews. But employers, especially less elite large firms and mid-size firms, generally recognize the need to maintain relationships with a wide variety of schools as they will never be able to obtain their associates from a small set of schools.

However, law firms affirmatively reach out to and recruit students at schools in the 100-200 range much, much less. Generally, most students at these schools, even those who do well, will have to obtain employment by identifying individual firms with open positions or otherwise interested in employing a new attorney and applying privately the old-fashioned way. Only perhaps the top 5% or so will have the opportunity to join large firms that are available to students at more well-regarded schools.

Side Note: Why Focus on Large Law Firms?

Why do those evaluating law student recruitment focus so much attention on large law firms - what's wrong with getting a nice job at a small or mid-size firm? While students at elite schools enjoy a relatively passive method of getting a job through on-campus interviews and summer associate programs, seemingly, what's so bad about applying individually to mid-size and smaller firms until one receives a permanent offer? Such a process is typical for students in almost every non-legal industry, and just involves somewhat more work than the more passive experience of landing a job out of a top law school. In addition, even if large law firms are out of the question, many students would be very happy working at mid-size or relatively small law firms.

However, as explained below, if you don't have a chance at landing a job at a large law firm, your chances of obtaining an entry-level employment as a lawyer becomes precarious.

Explaining why this is so significant requires explaining the somewhat unique aspects of entry-level legal recruiting as opposed to other industries. At the top of the market sits elite large law firms. These law firms have an annual need for many new associates. This is purposeful on their part and due to two fundamental and consistent aspects of the business models of these firms. First, these firms look to develop clients and new business that involves legal matters requiring large teams of partners and associates. They do this because they only want to have partners devote time to matters where they can also utilize and bill for the time of many associates. As a result, at many of these firms, there are many times the number of associates as partners.

Second, these firms rely on constant associate attrition to ensure this ratio, with as little as a couple percentage points of new associates being chosen for permanent positions such as partner or counsel. This leaves the firm with an annual need to refresh the ranks of junior associates. As mentioned above, several of these firms bring upwards of 100 new associates every year to serve as summer associates. In turn, these firms generally provide full-time offers of employment to a majority or even the vast majority of summer associates.

When you think about it, this business model is, on some level, an extraordinarily risky one, because if the firm is not able to refill a significant amount of its junior associate ranks, its ability to fulfill client demands and make money off associate leverage would be significantly imperiled. However, to elite firms, this is only a relatively minor risk because such firms have such a prestigious reputation that law students flock en masse to apply to these firms. As a result, these firms' only question is how top-tier their summer associate class is (and it is typically very top-tier, with, as mentioned above, more than 50% of summer associates attending one of the top five law schools), not whether they will fill it at all.

Their lead is followed by less elite but still large firms - i.e. the top 100 or 200 law firms by size. These firms depend on new associates to provide leverage but cannot, due to their somewhat less prestigious reputation, depend on constant attrition of almost all associates. These firms recruit every year, but the classes of new associates at these firms are only a fraction of the size of those at the elite firms.

For mid-size and small firms - firms more within the reach and interest of students at third tier law schools - recruiting becomes much more unclear and scattershot. Many of these firms do not have annual recruiting programs for new associates at all and the way they do recruit is more piecemeal and strategic. Rather than hire entry-level associates, many mid-size and small firms hire mid-level associates who have been trained at big law firms and are looking to leave. Many small firms have only a couple of associates, if that. These firms recruit if and when they have a specific need, may not look for an entry-level associate, and even if they are willing to accept an entry-level associate, may only be willing to provide a very small salary and poor benefits, even if the workload is heavy. You have student loans? These firms couldn't care less; they have to run a business with relatively small margins and have a thousand other applicants desperate for the job they are offering if you turn them down.

3. How to Apply to Your Situation

The above dealt with applying in the abstract. Of course, the ultimate goal here is extraordinarily specific, not to go to any law school, but particular ones that will supercharge your career.

By the time you apply, you will have a good idea about the makeup of the objective portions of your application - your GPA and your LSAT score. You may have your actual LSAT score in hand or you will have a general idea, based on practice tests, in what range you are likely to score. Given that law schools clearly indicate the scores and GPA attained by admitted students between the 25th and 75th percentile, many applicants are drawn to apply to the schools where they fit within those bands.

As an initial matter, I urge you to open up your options and apply to schools that you don't believe you have good chance of getting accepted to. The 25th percentile of students hitting a certain range means that a full 24%

of students admitted (if you are applying to law school because you are really, really bad at math, that's about 1 of every 4 students) to that school had lower numbers. Imagine what the students in the 1st percentile received.

Did you get that score? Then consider applying. You may get in, and even if you don't, you're only out a few dollars. The uniformity of law school applications makes submitting to numerous schools quite easy, and the application fee, while annoying, is an extraordinarily small pittance compared to the potential rewards from getting into a school with better opportunities.

Even more than not placing too much trust in percentile ranges, do not for a second doubt your ability to compete in a "reach" school. Some students indeed seemed to lack the ability to compete against so many other highly intelligent and driven students, but I believe that was a function of their drive and grit, not necessarily their LSAT scores or innate intelligence.

Related to "reach" schools and admissions based on criteria other than objective scores and grades, the question of to what extent applicants are admitted in part based on diversity is the elephant in the room. Certainly, many, if not most, law schools state an aspirational ideal of creating an academic community of numerous backgrounds. It is well known that such schools, like undergraduate schools and many other academic institutions, seek diversity by race, ethnicity and national origin.

What is less well known is that many law schools in particular, including perhaps all of the most elite law schools, also seek other types of diversity. One of the most prevalent is "geographic diversity." Simply put, a law school is more likely to admit applicants from parts of the country that are underrepresented at the school regardless of their socioeconomic, racial, ethnic or national origin background. It is harder to gain admission to an elite law school in New York when you are from New York than if you are from West Virginia. From what I understand, this criterion is based on two thoughts. -The first is a generalized diversity rationale, like other types of admissions based in part on diversity, to create a more heterogeneous student body. -The second is to help broaden the reach of the law school to parts of the country that may be less familiar with it. Another type of diversity sought by some schools is diversity in terms of age.

For you, this means that if you have anything unique to offer a law school, this is all the more reason to apply to shoot for the stars and apply to a meaningful amount of "reach" schools.

D. Where - to Accept

By this point, you have put in all of the hard work of applying, and the even harder work of then doing nothing other than anxiously checking your mailbox for the replies. Probably, your heart has been broken at least once by a "skinny letter," but hopefully at least once buoyed by a "big letter" of acceptance. If you receive multiple acceptances, the question of which one to accept will arise.

How should you evaluate these three factors and determine which school to attend, if any? Given the astronomical tuition that many law schools charge, making this decision will ultimately come down to an individualized question of each person's risk tolerance, i.e. how much risk capital, in terms of tuition, you are willing to risk in exchange for more potential rewards from a better school. By going to a higher-ranked school even if a lower-ranked school is cheaper or offers you a scholarship, you are taking on more risk in terms of more debt based on the potential for higher reward in terms of better entry-level opportunities as well as better opportunities throughout your career. I don't offer any specific rules to follow because the results of the risk tolerance you select are highly individualized and idiosyncratic to your situation.

However, I do believe there are three general principles I would argue prudent potential lawyers should follow.

First, if you are able to obtain a full or substantial guaranteed scholarship to a "national" school, you should accept that offer rather than attending a slightly more prestigious national school. Similarly, if you are able to obtain a full or substantial guaranteed scholarship to a "regional" school within the same geographic area and within the same band of other regional schools to which you have also been accepted, you should take it. Your options will only go marginally down; the highly reduced tuition will allow you to start your legal career on a solid footing, you hopefully will excel in the lower-ranked school, and you can explain the less prestige by putting the scholarship on your resume.

Second, another general rule is that if you only qualify for a regional school, try to go to a lower-ranked school within your geographic area that provides at least half scholarship (if guaranteed for three years). Given that it is a regional school, your chances of obtaining employment sufficient to justify full tuition are already shaky, so you owe it to your future self to not risk it all on the potential to hit it big.

Third, I would argue that if you already have a good job, it does not make sense to go to regional schools ranked below a certain point, approximately those lower than the 50-60 range, without a full or very substantial scholarship. At that point, these schools offer a very shaky opportunity to obtain lucrative legal work, and if you already are making $40,000 or $50,000, you have many years to achieve satisfaction and financial success in your career without the anchors of high debt and a law degree that can limit as much as it advances.

Beyond that, these are personal decisions based on your goals, how narrow or broad they are, and how much risk you are willing to tolerate both in terms of debt load and the risk of not gaining sufficient entry-level employment. Let's take a few New York City case studies by way of (extraordinarily provincial) example.

a. Should you turn down Harvard or Yale for a meaningful scholarship to NYU? Yes, you will have lower debt, and largely the same entry-level opportunities, but you will never have a Y- or H-bomb, and there is no equivalent S-bomb for "Well, I got a big scholarship." You may think it was a great deal for the first 3 years of your career, but rue it in year 10. Or not.

b. Should you turn down Columbia for a full scholarship to Fordham? Sounds like a good deal. If you do reasonably well you should be able to land a job at a large law firm in New York City, with a clean financial profile that will allow you to spend your earnings on what you want rather than interest payments. However, if you're dead-set on working at an uber-elite firm, you simply may not achieve your goals. What about a half scholarship?

c. Same question for turning down Fordham (or Columbia) for Brooklyn Law? Here, your opportunity set has skewed strongly against big firms, plum clerkships, and government jobs, and you will have to do extraordinarily well to have such opportunities. If you are confident in your abilities to do so, then this may be the best gamble you ever made. If you finish in the bottom half of your class, you may have to scramble to land even the lowest-paying jobs, or any job.

Ultimately, as a lawyer, you will be entrusted with transactions, litigations, and other important and confidential matters that require the highest level of sensitivity, prudence, and thought. Making a decision on where to go to law school or whether to go at all, as hard as that decision is, may be your easiest decision in comparison.

E. When

1. ...to Apply

The answer to the question of when to apply is simple: As soon as possible in the normal application cycle in which you are submitting the majority of your applications. Law schools generally run rolling admission cycles during a set time period, typically starting in September or October of the year before one would begin school and continuing until a couple of months or even a matter of weeks before the actual school year starts. While it is true that law schools consider and admit a large number of applicants throughout the cycle, certainly it can only help for your application to be considered before a large percentage of the class has already been offered admission and/or accepted such offer. I have previously noted related advice to prepare the important pieces of your application, such as your essay, your LSAT, and your recommendations even before the application cycle opens. If you do so, you will be able to submit close to the beginning of the cycle and get the committee's attention unsullied by a large number of prior applicants.

2. ...to Accept?

A question related to the previous question regarding which school to accept if you have multiple offers is when to do so. Should you accept soon after receipt or try to land another offer at a better school? To start, there is certainly no harm in sending a very short, professional note to the admissions committee of your school of choice noting your acceptance elsewhere. However, keep in mind that most schools receive many applications and they will not be concerned about losing particular students. The note will help if they are leaning towards accepting you already, but it will not provide independent sway, so make sure to not imply any arrogance in your communication.

Beyond that, at some point you will have to accept. Law schools do accept students throughout the year and up to the week before classes start, but generally they will accept less and less as time goes on. You should make the decision based on the expectation that you will not receive any additional offers.

In making your decision, you need to be your own best advocate - your own lawyer, if you will. Law schools are huge institutions run by wealthy, successful people that are designed to process (and sometimes prey on) hundreds of young people per year. Ask questions. Law schools aren't used car salesmen, but they aren't your parents either.

PART 2
Law School

Chapter 5: First Year

Welcome to law school! Law school will be an academic experience unlike any you have had before. Law school is definitely not the most challenging type of academic institution - it doesn't hold a candle to medical school and many others - but it will be a unique time in your life where you are alternatively engaged, stressed out, or bored (perhaps, all at the same time) more than you ever have before.

Moreover, your wide-eyed introduction will be short, as the first year is by far the most important in law school and perhaps in your legal career. Succeeding academically in your first year of law school is likely of greater relative importance to the rest of your time at school than any other academic program.

Thus, a thoughtful plan is critical. This chapter analyzes the three most important aspects of the first year. First, I dissect how to approach the year academically, including how to approach class, studying during the semester and for finals, and qualifying for law review. Second, I discuss law school life and the crucial importance of socializing. Third, more soft skills - how to deal with professors, which, even if your school has anonymous tests, is crucially important.

1. Academics

During your first year, you will take courses in basic aspects of US law, likely including most or all of the following: torts, contracts, legal writing, property, constitutional law, civil procedure, and criminal law. Your grades in these courses will be the most important determination as to what jobs you can obtain after law school. Given both this point in addition to the fact that many times your entry-level position will play a major role in what jobs you can obtain later on in your legal career, clearly first-year grades are extraordinarily important. Are they everything? No, like an LSAT score isn't everything. But, like the LSAT, they are crucial.

You will quickly learn what these courses involve in school and don't need a guide for that. How I can help is to provide you with several ways to approach classes and studying in a smarter, strategic way.

a. Reading

The first aspect of law school that you will find different from your other academic endeavors is the unique textbook provided to you. For many of your college classes featuring a particular topic leading to a final exam, you were likely provided with a textbook with expository material in prose leading you through the topic systematically. By and large, law school casebooks fail to do that. Instead, they provide full text or edited versions of actual decisions issued by judges related to that particular topic. Frequently, the book provides very little of the actual legal doctrine and interpretations other than summary snippets, relatively vague allusions and questions to ponder regarding the quoted cases.

What results from this is that in law school, you have to teach yourself to some extent. Instead of just having to remember material, you will have to piece it together yourself from the original sources, with the help of your professors. In addition, you will have to derive the rules of law from the cases themselves. This is because US law is common law-based, meaning that the doctrines are created and continually developed by courts, especially in the first-year courses like contracts and torts where there are relatively little statutes and regulations involved. This is opposed to the European civil law system, where the sources of legal rules are statutes and rules, and courts merely decide where a case falls when the rules are applied.

Prior to understanding and analyzing cases, it's helpful to understand the basic makeup of almost any well-written legal opinion. The first section is factual background, where the judge recites the facts that he or she has chosen to accept or that have been accepted by the parties at that stage in the proceedings. The decision will then explain the "procedural posture" or the prior history of the case in the courts. The decision should then lay out, if it has not already done so, the precise question that the court is answering and the impact that the decision will make. The next section is the analysis section. This is broken down into two sub-sections. First, the court lays out the relevant legal rules. Second, the court applies those rules to the facts. Ultimately, the court will reach a conclusion and issue an order to the parties and, if the court is an appeals court, the lower court.

Given that many of these cases can be numerous pages long, with a long, winding background and a lot of back and forth in the analysis section, what is the best way to systematically attack case readings? First, the background section is just that - background. Don't feel the need to get bogged down in the back and forth of the disputes between the parties as to what had occurred and the procedural history, as these sections are merely a means to the end of applying the law. You will need to understand the background to see how the judge is applying the legal rules. More practically, if you know the basic thrust of the facts of each case, you will be able to recognize when a professor inserts similar facts into a fact pattern underlying a law school exam question. While the professor will likely not be looking for you to simply apply the exact rule of law coming out of the case involving the similar facts, but rather slightly changing the facts to yield a potentially different rule of law, it will be helpful to orient yourself in the question by knowing that that case is likely relevant in some way. In addition, if less practically, the facts are usually the most interesting part of opinions. Thus, it's good to read and retain a basic overview of the facts, but feel free to read them relatively quickly.

The legal analysis section is where you should be spending most of your time, and to properly attack this section, there is a well-known approach to law school exams called the IRAC method. You should be flexible in your exam answers based on the professor's guidance, but IRAC is a great method to efficiently attacking case law in readings.

What is IRAC? Under IRAC, one can break down every case into four parts:

- an <u>Issue</u>, the legal question at hand.

- a generalized legal <u>Rule</u> to apply regarding the issue, with the specifics of how to apply the rule unclear in this case.
- an <u>Application</u> of the generalized Rule to the facts at issue, and
- a <u>Conclusion</u> of law resulting from the application.

All four parts of this analysis will take place in the analysis section of the opinion. Derive and highlight the four parts to IRAC in the opinion. Try to only highlight the precise points that ultimately win out, without identifying every potential rule and application if the opinion engages in a lot of back and forth.

After reading the case, you will likely not have a complete understanding of it and especially where it lies in the context of a broader area of law. That is what class and future study are for. But even reaching a basic understanding of your first cases is a tremendous accomplishment, and hopefully feels good too. Bask in that glory a bit before you read the next case.

As studying and understanding original cases may seem daunting at first, keep in mind that there are several aspects of your reading that you will not have to focus on and can largely set aside. Many case books will have extended chapter introductions providing the historical context for the doctrines, even going back to English common law. These introductions are completely irrelevant, although perhaps fascinating. Moreover, as mentioned above, procedural history and posture are frequently complicated and luckily you will never be expected to apply such issues in your exams - law school exams are doctrinal exams, not litigation primers. In addition, in your legal writing class, you may be asked to read reams of material that you will not be tested on; while you may be expected in such classes to occasionally participate and thus should have some understanding of this material, generally you should be able to read this material very quickly as well. Finally, many case books will provide material explaining minor quirks in the law of particular subjects; generally, if a professor never covers a particular quirk, you can safely assume that quirk will not be on an exam.

b. Class

The second unique aspect of law school is the unique role of classroom time. Especially given that students are expected to make sure to independently understand the cases and how they fit together, the question could be asked: what is the purpose of class? In many college classes, attendance at every class is not particularly necessary if you are able to understand the material. Is law school the same way? Conventional wisdom is that attendance in law school is indeed paramount, and you will usually see very few if any empty seats during class, even if participation is not important. Is this another myth requiring a good busting?

Here, I believe that the conventional wisdom is correct - attending law school classes, preferably every single one, is indeed very important to excel in a course. This is because most law school exams do not simply require understanding the material. Rather, each professor will expect fealty to his or her unique understanding of the area of law and how the cases fit together. The more you track the professor's weltanschauung and interpretation, even in terms of the precise words the professor uses to describe the cases, the more the professor will agree with your explanation. This is no doubt part intentional on the professor's part and part subconscious given the psychological reality that we like people more like ourselves and who agree with ourselves. The more you parrot the professor, the more the professor will simply "like" your exam. Given the highly discretionary method of grading which most professors follow, you owe it to yourself to put yourself on the professor's "good" side. To be clear, this doesn't mean you have to agree with the professor's policy ideas or criticisms of the case, but you do need to zero in on how the professor views the case objectively within the context of the legal doctrine.

Attending class is, in turn, the best way to understand how the professor views the law and how the cases fit together. Your main goal in class should be to identify how the professor frames each case, what conclusions does he or she glean from that case, and how he or she places the case in the context of the other cases as well the general legal doctrine underlying the area of law. The good professors will make their conclusions clear, while with others you will, unfortunately, have to intensely focus to derive the ultimate lessons relevant to an exam, and still other professors simply prattle on and you will ultimately have to teach yourself.

However, I believe there are two ways in which the conventional wisdom regarding class is incorrect - one aspect of class that people think is important but is not, and another that people don't appreciate the importance.

First, what everyone thinks is important: Doing well when called on by a professor. Law school classes are famous for being intimidating. The Socratic method, whereby a professor randomly selects individual students and aggressively questions them regarding cases and requires them to engage in a dialogue, was memorialized in the class movie, The Paper Chase. However, it's important to ignore the urge to stress out about class and being called on, as class participation is much less important than you think. In many law school classes, class participation is completely irrelevant, and 100% of your grades will depend on your performance on the final exam. In most classes, class participation is at best a very slight mover of a grade when a student is on the border. Even when it is relevant to that extent, professors will be assessing whether you participated in class by participating in the discussion occasionally by asking questions or offering your viewpoint, not grading you on your performance in response to questions.

Ultimately, professors all know that the Socratic method is new to law students. They continue it, perhaps out of blind fealty to tradition or perhaps based on the view that it is good training for the type of questioning you will receive from a judge, but they do not expect anyone to excel. Yes, certainly be sure to read the cases before class so you have some ability to engage in discussion, but you should be doing that anyway.

Second, one aspect of class that people view as not problematic is using the Internet or otherwise using a computer for something other than taking notes. This is an extremely bad idea.[17] The vast majority of professors won't care and everyone does it, but it may make a significant dent in your grades. As discussed above, the whole point of class, besides reading the case book, is to understand the way the professor thinks about the legal doctrine, his or her unique take on each major case, and how he or she evaluates each case in the context of other cases and the legal doctrine. These are not quick factoids for which you can quickly tune in and subsequently tune out. Rather, it is something you can only understand by focusing on the professor, any more than you can relate to any human being's unique perspective while buried in a device.

My advice? Don't ever take an electronic device to class. Yes, it is much more convenient to take notes on a computer. However, that convenience is far outweighed by the enticement to distraction that these devices cause to you. You will look weird in classes that don't ban electronic devices. Your classmates may comment or even snicker. They can snicker in the unemployment line too. If you must bring an electronic device for note-taking, put the device in airline mode. If you find yourself wanting to turn airline mode off, junk the device and get a pen and pad. Relax, this isn't med school. There's only so much you'll have to write down anyway.

My final piece of advice regarding class participation is a way to mitigate the way you stand out by not having an electronic device. One way to do that is not to get involved in too many contentious debates. Law school courses, especially in the first year when students are highly competitive, involve well-known areas of the law such as torts, criminal law, and constitutional law, regarding which many law students have strong opinions. Some students become emotionally attached to their opinions on these subjects and many discussions in law school courses devolve into heated debate.

For many reasons, you might want to consider limiting your involvement in these debates.[18] Of course, there is zero benefit practically to your academic success. Further, your opinions may antagonize other students who are

---

[17] Robert Miller makes this point in <u>Law School Confidential</u>.
[18] Miller, Law School Confidential, *supra*.

emotionally attached to opposing opinions. Finally, especially if you opine too frequently, students may simply hate your guts for wasting their time and sounding like a talk radio host.

Some readers may view my advice as overly cautious, even cowardly. I'm certainly not saying that you should censor yourself. Yes, academic environments are a perfect place to express your views on these subjects. However, law school classes are frequently overheated by these debates, as they become overly emotional and can be as juvenile as a Facebook comment debate. At the end of the day, participating is fine if you truly enjoy it, but don't expect to accomplish anything, and certainly don't expect to convince anyone.

This advice applies generally, but especially applies to politically charged discussions, of which there will be many. Again, I'm not saying you should not participate, or be afraid to voice opinions with which even the majority of your fellow students will disagree, but do everything in moderation. At the very least, before you speak, think at length about what you intend to say. Summarily prepare your remarks and consider whether they will add to the discussion. I consider myself a relatively non-judgmental person with relatively moderate political positions, but the impression made by those students who, time and time again, took extreme, almost outlandish positions on charged issues is quite indelible. If I came across them in a professional setting, it would be difficult to take them seriously, and even more so to offer them business or a job.

c. Outlines

As the semester continues and you adjust to school and your methods, you may feel a sense of accomplishment building. You are understanding the material, you get along with the professor and even did relatively well under Socratic scrutiny once or twice, and, while you'd rather be tanning in Miami, you are - dare say it - even enjoying law school.

Wipe that smile from your face. While panic is bad, just as bad is a false sense of accomplishment. Don't be fooled - until the final exam, you have accomplished exactly nothing. To use a phrase probably familiar to you from the LSAT, final exams are both necessary and sufficient conditions to succeeding in law school. Everything else is whipped cream.

To prepare for finals, you will need to construct an outline providing the framework for your understanding of the material covered during the semester. Go back to your distilled versions of each case. Armed with the background and insight provided by class and later cases, you may realize that some of your prior understanding was simply incomplete and lacking in context and sophistication, and you should update accordingly. Of course, you'll also realize that some of your prior notes were nonsense. That's what the semester is for - appreciate how far you have grown in your understanding of the law.

Construct an outline of the ultimate legal framework and place each case in the proper context. In the same outline, you should also include those interpretations from your professor that are relevant to a case or series of cases when such interpretations add materially to the legal rule and applications emerging from the case.

As you may feel overwhelmed and lost in creating a proprietary outline, some assistance is helpful. Feel free to consult one of the many commercial outlines available to law students, especially to provide the basic building blocks of particular areas of law and to help in understanding particularly difficult cases. You may find the outlines of other students helpful.

However, I urge you to create your own outline from scratch and suppress the urge to simply take a template or slightly modify an outline from a book or from a classmate. This is for three reasons.

First, trust no one. The reality is that many of your classmates are dumb and haven't read this book. Their outlines are materially deficient. In all seriousness, there is no particular reason to believe any of your classmates are smarter than you or have a better grasp of the material. In law school, many of my classmates who appeared to be extremely bright and capable did relatively poorly in law school, while those who seemed the opposite attained the highest honors and job opportunities.

Second, as mentioned above, preparing for a final is a custom attempt to get inside your professor's brain. A commercial outline will not help at all in that endeavor, and may interpret cases significantly differently than your professor. Other students may be equally clueless. Third, creating the outline will itself help you form a bond with the material and help you sort through it mentally.

d. Finals

Study your outline significantly and know it inside and out. Construction of your outline will take a while, so you should allocate a meaningful amount of time to it, at least a couple of weeks, and still allow sufficient time for studying the outline prior to finals.

However, aim to study strategically and not simply pound material. Do not feel the need to over study. The difference between law and other graduate programs is that law is ultimately an intellectual program dependent on analysis, and not rote memory or application. It is easy to fall into the trap of pounding outlines and cases more and more obscure out of the concern that the professor may bring up a case you have not reviewed.

Resist the urge. Instead, focus on two methods of smarter studying focused on the precise class you are taking. The first such method is practicing writing answers to exam questions. If your professor provides exemplars from previous tests, take as many as you can fit into your schedule. Each one will enhance your understanding of the professor's thought process and the types of questions and areas of law that the professor covers on exams.

The second such method is to attend any review sessions graciously provided by your professor. At these sessions, take in every word uttered with bated breath. Listen carefully to the answers the professor provides to questions and ask your own. Hopefully, your professor will *sua sponte*[19] provide a general overview of how he or she approaches test questions and what types of answers he or she is looking for. If not, ask.

In the week immediately prior to finals and during finals week, keep calm and again avoid the urge to panic and over-study. By this point, you truly either know it or you don't, and thinking you are not fully understanding some tiny detail probably just means that you know it. Be sure to get plenty of sleep for the two nights prior to every exam, given that evidence shows that fatigue can be caused by lack of sleep two nights before even more than the night before, and you probably won't be able to sleep that well the night before anyway.

Be sure to arrive at the test site plenty of time before the exam, make sure you have backup power in the event of technical difficulties, and good luck!

2. Law School Life

a. Socializing

Law school social life and getting to know your fellow students is an important part of the law school experience that every law student should take advantage of for many reasons, in addition to simply being an enjoyable activity. To begin, law school is a serious, at times overly serious, place. Regularly socializing, laughing about whatever overly serious exchange happened in class, or simply having a good time provides a needed reversal of the feelings of anxiety, inferiority and even panic that can creep into your psyche over a semester, especially during the first year.

Second, law school is by far the best networking opportunity you will ever have. Simply the ability to hang around hundreds of potential future clients and contacts for job opportunities is a great opportunity. By way of explanation, let me compare the law school networking opportunity to your future networking opportunities in a few ways.

---

[19] If you don't know this phrase yet you are going to fail – for absence of doubt, in love and in life, in addition to your law school finals.

First, your future self will likely be paying thousands of dollars for conferences, lunches, sports tickets and the like simply to meet or entertain one or a few such persons at a time for a few hours at a time, while law school provides this benefit free with your tuition, extends it to hundreds of people and for three years of academic study.

In addition, your future self where networking will be done in relatively cold, professional settings, where everyone ultimately realizes they are there only for professional reasons. Due to this professional overlay, any relationships are slow to start and grow equally slow, except for the rare occurrences when people truly hit it off. Contrast this with your experience at law school, where you will have the opportunity to forge close, non-professional relationships with your fellow students and grow to truly enjoy each other's company. It is these types of relationships that can be extraordinarily beneficial over time.

While the above analysis may sound cynical or even creepy (oh great, you're just drinking with us because he sees us as future clients … yeah let's make an excuse to get out of here), I don't mean to imply that you should approach law school socializing in any cold or calculating way. Simply have fun, assuming you know how to do that sort of thing.

Ultimately, I'm not arguing for any particular type of socializing; The only specific approach that I would argue for is to get to know a wide variety of people and not exclusively stick to a tiny clique. I'm just arguing that you should not avoid socializing due to concerns that you cannot afford to do so due to studying. At the end of the day, law school is hard work, but as mentioned previously it is not, or at least should not be if you are approaching it correctly, an extraordinarily taxing exercise involving the constant cramming, all-nighters and the like that, for example, medical school may entail. You should have time to socialize. Indeed, far from not being able to afford to do so, you really cannot afford not to. In addition to the obvious meals, get-togethers, parties, and the like, take advantage of any academic or extracurricular opportunities to work with other students, especially those interested in similar niches, such as in clubs, committees, or law review work.

b. Competition

On the opposite side of socializing, it's also necessary to bring up the perhaps unique atmosphere of competition that pervades many first-year law school classes. While law schools vary in how students display and deal with competition, competition is ultimately a structural fixture of every law school. Many law school classes are graded on fixed curves. Law reviews have a fixed amount of spaces. Law firms and judges are only hiring so many students. Your fellow law students are directly competing with you in a zero sum game for grades and ultimately job offers.

How you choose to react to that reality is, however, another issue entirely. My view is an honest but civil approach. On the one hand, at some point you do need to stick out for your own interest. You don't have to share your outlines, although I did, and received many in return. You don't have to study with students who are not helpful to you.

On the other hand, actual competitive behavior or speech is counterproductive. You will do well in your finals because you study well, not because of poor behavior in or out of class vis-à-vis other students; the only thing that such behavior will result in is ruining your reputation among your law school class of future clients and contacts.

There are a few ways to apply this attitude in practice. First, avoid being a "gunner" in class. Every first-year law school class features a few students who are either extremely passionate about everything the professors talk about, love hearing themselves talk, or (more likely) are insecure and feel the need to prove their self-worth to others in a rare setting that is both relatively public but provides few clear negative consequences for talking excessively. Professors frequently need students to fill the silence and many of them don't enjoy cold-calling any more than the students do. Thus, you could even argue that serving as a gunner is a public service that involves helping out professors and students alike.

At the end of the day, though, serving as a gunner will result in certain negative consequence of many of your fellow students believing you to be an amoeba with a mouth attached. Remember, these are your future clients and contacts. No one is saying you have to be a conformist, but there is a time and place for everything. Unless you have close friends in law school, there is no bartender in class to tell you that you've had enough.

In contrast to these certain negative consequences, there is little to nothing positive that can emerge from transforming into *homo gunnerus*. Of course, being a gunner will not improve your grades at all, where they are based exclusively on exams. Even in those classes where class participation can potentially raise a grade, the only participation necessary is occasional; no professor will provide students with improved grades for frequent participation and certainly not for participating in every class. I know many gunners who evidently did relatively poorly in classes, while many extremely quiet students excelled and reaped the rewards. In terms of relating to professors as well, a much better way for professors to form a positive view of you is through personal, private interaction rather than simply raising your hand all the time.

Another suggestion to reducing competition is not to sweat the small stuff. Some of your fellow students will, whether with malintent or simply due to their personality disorders, attempt to intimidate you or compare themselves to you and other students. Keep your eyes on the prize - good grades on exams you take by yourself. Everything else is noise. For example, many law schools will have required projects that are pass-fail or are otherwise not important to one's grades. Avoid becoming competitive with other students on such projects. I'm not at all saying to avoid doing the required work, but again, keep your eyes on what is important.

c. Working and Living with Other Students

Another question related to law school life is how to structure group study or living with other students. While there are no clear answers here, I believe that, as opposed to socializing, some caution should be taken here. While many students organize study groups and appear to assume that they are necessary, they're not, and I believe you should spend only a limited amount of time with such groups. To be sure, for those students that are truly not understanding the material, these groups will help with that, although treatises and commercial outlines can as well. Speaking occasionally with other students to get broader points, fill in gaps, exchange outlines and notes and discuss exam preparation is also generally helpful.

But in most instances for most people, these groups are largely a waste of time. Indeed, in some cases, such as if your group mates are the competitive or panicky types or uninformed, they may also be affirmatively bad and damage your confidence or preparedness. So proceed with caution.

Living in a law student-centered arrangement is also something that should give you some pause. On the one hand, living on campus in student housing will make it easier to get to know your fellow students in addition to being generally convenient. However, as mentioned previously, the atmospheres of many law schools can become toxic, especially near finals. Even if you share an apartment or house with fellow students, choosing to avoid formal student housing may allow you to escape that atmosphere and provide for a more relaxed atmosphere conducive to proper study. You also may want to consider not studying in your room or house for similar reasons.

d. Living Expenses

A related point is the financial impact of deciding whether to live on or off-campus, and in general how much to pay for living expenses. Federal loan guidelines allow graduate students to borrow for living expenses, and there is a significant availability of private loans for such expenses. The fact that these funds are available serves as a siren call of sorts for many students, especially those who are confident in their ability to secure excellent post-graduation employment, to borrow freely and live comfortably, if not luxuriously. Law schools are fully aware of this, providing students with comfortable student living facilities, convenient food service, and other amenities.

However, assuming you are taking out debt to pay living expenses, I highly encourage you to minimize your living expenses as much as possible and push furiously against the instinct to borrow more. You need to remind yourself that the more loans you take out, the worse your post-graduation financial situation will be, even if you secure good employment.

Two points in particular are helpful to try to illustrate this. First, remember that these loans are not interest-free - you may need to pay back several dollars for every extra dollar you borrow over the course of a loan. Second, you will be paying these loans back with post-tax income, and if your household makes sufficient income, you will not be able to deduct the interest expense either.

To plug in real numbers, let's say you take out an additional $10,000 in living expenses per year more than you absolutely needed to. Even disregarding the interest that accrues during law school, assuming a 20-year payoff schedule and a 6% rate, you would have to pay back over $21,000 in interest over the life of the loan and would have to pay an additional $2500 per year in payments, requiring up to $5,000 in additional post-tax income per year to fund the additional payments.

Ultimately, I urge you, assuming you are borrowing, to eat in, find a cheap apartment, if necessary off-campus, and generally look to keep your expenses low. If you wouldn't take out credit card debt to live more comfortably, why would you take out student loans?

Two counterarguments are generally offered to this advice. First, some may legitimately worry that living so frugally may isolate one from the other students. As mentioned above, it is a great idea to stay connected with other law students, both simply for your own sanity and enjoyment as well as for the social and networking opportunities. To be clear, my advice doesn't mean you can't have a social life - by all means go to parties and get a ride or take public transportation home. Normal law students shouldn't look askance at you for brown-bagging it rather than buying from the law school cafeteria. Another potential objection is that law students need every convenience they can get to invest all of their energy into studying. I simply disagree with this one. As outlined previously, law school is not the type of all-in effort like perhaps some other academic endeavors that others make it out to be. Even with taking numerous efforts to save money, you will have much more than enough study time to ace all of your courses. Perhaps, a few minutes studying on a train instead of on your bed, but your future self will be grateful for decades for the prudence you showed for three years.

3. Dealing with Professors

Forging relationships with professors is very important. As opposed to the extremely normal way in which you should interact with your classmates, with your professors, you should definitely ensure that they like you. While your first-year grades, assuming your school works on a blind basis, will not be dependent on the subjective discretion of the professor, relationships with professors pay off in several other ways. First, clerkships and some government jobs require letters of recommendation from professors. These letters can buoy your candidacy much more than with regard to law school admissions. For clerkships, good grades are a must, for sure, but any judge offering a prestigious clerkship will receive numerous applications containing equally impressive grades. Judges trust the judgment of law school professors, especially those they know personally, with whose work they are familiar or who they otherwise know to be prominent. In turn, while professors will generally always write positive letters for high-achieving students, a letter written for someone with whom the professor has a genuine relationship is usually fundamentally distinct from the vague generalities in letters for students who are simply one of the crowd.

There are other reasons to form relationships with professors even for those who are not interested in such opportunities:

- Professors have discretion over all sorts of awards, fellowships, and other opportunities provided by the law school.

- Working for a well-known professor as a research assistant during the summer after your first year of law school is a prestigious appointment that will reflect well as you go for interview during your second year.

- You may also gain the opportunity to serve as a teacher's assistant in your second or third year, do pro bono work with the professor or co-author a law review article with him or her, which will also enhance your resume.

Finally, professors may be, in many cases, great mentors for your nascent legal career. They will have a large rolodex of contacts and may have previously worked in the same type of corporate, law firm, government or organizational work you are looking to enter. If you form a noteworthy bond, this relationship may even bear fruit years down the line. Best of all, these relationships are, like the socializing opportunities, completely free and included as part of your tuition. With nothing to lose, and a relatively minimal time investment, getting to know professors is a no-brainer.

How to form a relationship with professors, many of whom are not exactly social butterflies? There is obviously no single path and professors have varied personalities, but a few suggestions are in order. In addition to trying your best at Socratic dialogue and asking the occasional question in class, be sure to speak occasionally after class or during office hours with professors with whom you potentially see a relationship starting. Ask questions on the material, even policy or other questions not necessarily needed for doing well on the exam, or on the best approach to studying the cases. Resist the feeling that your questions are more easily directed to a reference book, that you are wasting the professor's time, or that your communications are disingenuous given your ulterior motives. Yes, this is all a game. Professors know that they are not friends with their students, but this is ultimately their job. Many professors enjoy student interaction; remember, they will otherwise be sitting at their desk by themselves for long stretches of time with no companion other than the federal administrative precedent for regulating beaver habitats. You can beat that.

In addition to taking time to develop a personal relationship, also look for opportunities to work together. In your second and/or third year, jump at the chance to turn your writing assignment into a law review article co-written with your professor. Moreover, flattery always helps - while you should feel free to take positions in class, avoid taking a clear opinion directly opposite to your professor's strongest-held beliefs, either in class or in discussions. Ultimately, you should treat professors somewhat like you'd treat a boss, and securing good relationships with them will bear almost as much fruit.

Chapter 6: First Summer

With the intellectual and competitive nature of your immersion into legal studies during the first year of law school, it is easy to lose track of the end game of gainful employment to which your studies are hopefully leading. This chapter helps you refocus back to this end game with an extended discussion on the summer after your first year of law school. This summer will be filled with consequential decisions and activities, including the law review competition, your first summer job, and other preparations for the second year. In this chapter, I discuss each of these issues, and provide advice on strategy for obtaining a solid first-summer job as well as a short discussion on ways you may want to prepare for the second year.

A. Law Review

Every law school of which I am aware produces an academic legal journal, referred to by most school as a law review. This publication collects submissions of legal scholarship, primarily from law professors and other legal scholars in addition to law students, and selects certain submissions for publication, ultimately producing one to five volumes per year. Law reviews are exclusively managed, edited, and produced by volunteer law students. Much of the work involved is extremely tedious and monotonous, and working for the law review or another law journal published by the school will take up a significant amount of time that could be used for employment, personal time, or studying.

Despite the effort required, I still urge each and every one of you to apply to your school's law review. Being selected to serve on a law review is the greatest honor accruing from one's time as a student one can have on a resume. The honor lives on throughout one's career, as law review membership signifies that one is, at once, very bright, diligent, and capable enough to withstand both the competition of getting on and the intense and detail-oriented demands entailed by service. Even if you did not attend an elite school, obtaining law review will still transform the law school section of your resume or biography to an impressive conversation piece.

I believe law review membership is helpful for a wide variety of law students - essentially everyone. For students at non-elite schools, law review membership may be required or extremely helpful to obtain a job at a large law firm. However, even students at elite law schools benefit immensely from having a law review credential on a resume. It opens up opportunities, from law firms (both on an entry-level and throughout one's career) to clerkships, to a wide variety of government and organizational jobs, to academic work. It distinguishes one from the thousands of other graduates of your school, including many who are likely applying for the same position that you are.

Working on a law review also provides very helpful networking, as you will have the opportunity to form close, semi-professional, semi-personal relationships with a cross-section of the school's best and brightest. These students will go on to a variety of successful careers, and it will serve you well to have gotten to know them well when you did.

It is due to these reasons that I recommend law review membership even for students who are certain that they want to practice corporate law. At the end of the day, you are in school anyway, so you might as well use your time wisely to prepare for your career, and you will likely not regret missing the binge-watching you could have done instead of cite-checking. (If anything, just binge-watch during the time you would have been studying for your second or third-year classes.)

A tougher question is whether to accept invitations to work on other student-edited law journals at the school if you are rejected from the school's flagship law review. Here, I would distinguish. If you are interested in clerkships, governmental work, litigation, or academia, then having a law journal credential is very helpful in demonstrating your interest and competence in the research and writing inherent in these positions. For many positions, such a credential may be officially or unofficially required.

In addition to serving as a credential, the practical work you will do on a law journal - editing complex legal writing and becoming an expert in legal citation - will be relevant skills for these professions.

However, if you are certain that you want to be a transactional or advisory attorney, there is much less reason to work on a journal. A second-tier law journal is of marginal quality as a credential. In addition, it is not particularly helpful practically given the lack of fit between the skills developed at the journal and the skills involved in these practice areas. To be sure, I would recommend that you involve yourself in some extra-curricular activity during law school to demonstrate that you are well-rounded. However, working on a law journal is a serious time commitment, and there are many other activities in which you could engage, such as getting involved in a student group, which may be more subjectively interesting to you, bear more relevance to your future career, and involve a lesser time commitment. Like many other ways in which law students and lawyers blindly conform, many students simply join a law journal because that is what everyone else at school is doing. At the end of the day you won't lose much other than time if you follow suit, but nevertheless don't feel obligated to.

B. Applying for First Year Jobs

Another important distraction from your first-year studies is applying for summer jobs available to law students between their first and second years of law school. This process is one of the more entrepreneurial and unstructured aspects of law school for many students. It is also an aspect that, while its importance can be overstated, is still important enough that law students are well-served to provide it sufficient diligence and care. Below, I provide suggestions both on how to conduct a search as well as how to decide what jobs to apply for and accept.

1. When

The first question is when to begin conducting your search. As opposed to second summer jobs, which begin with a fixed on-campus recruiting schedule, first summer jobs do not have any set schedule and frequently involve few to no on-campus interviews.

This lack of structure creates a question for students regarding when to begin the application process. Most schools adhere to policies prohibiting first-year students from applying for positions prior to November of the fall semester. Other than that, there are essentially no other limitations. Many students may be inclined to begin as soon as possible to avoid being stuck without a job while others may be concerned about interrupting their studies, especially since first year grades are the most important factor in obtaining a second summer job, which in turn is far more important than a first summer job.

Ultimately, I believe there is little to no reason to apply for jobs prior to completing your first semester finals in December. The vast majority of employers will not be interested in your application prior to that date. For those employers, such as large law firms, that have established summer programs seeking first-year law students, they need to review your first semester grades before making a decision. Even if the firms advertise positions during the first semester, their decision-making process is not rolling. They will generally be unable to make decisions until grades are received, and their decision or not to extend interview invitations will be based, except for certain programs which have explicit diversity preferences, overwhelmingly on those grades.

Buttressing these reasons that waiting will not hurt you, submitting numerous job applications during your first semester certainly will provide you with additional stress. Given the extraordinary importance of doing well during your first year, there is no reason to let even something like jobs distract you, especially since, as described above, there is little to no marginal benefit from getting started early.

If you do want to apply to get on these employers' radar, feel free to apply during winter break. However, you may want to push off applying even until the spring semester. You may legitimately want to relax during winter break, and waiting until your grades come in may save you a lot of wasted time spent applying in the event they are not positive enough to warrant a paid position at a large law firm.

In addition to the complications regarding when to apply, which is created by the system's lack of structure, the system also creates unique problems regarding when to accept a job. Given that job availability during your first year is so idiosyncratic, you may find yourself relatively early in the year with an offer for a job that, while it may be acceptable, is not your dream job.

Your approach here should be guided by three principles. First - realism. The reality is that it is very difficult to obtain certain types of first-year positions, such as a position as a summer associate in a large law firm. In addition, the reality is that as long as you are working as a lawyer during your first summer at a job where you can extract a couple of interesting tidbits for use in your second-year interviews, that is quite sufficient for the ultimate end game of obtaining quality post-law school employment. Assuming you are otherwise a relatively standard candidate, most law firms and other employers will not be overly judgmental on what employment you obtained during the first summer. Far more important are conversation skills during the interview and your grades.

Second, your application process should also be guided and limited by your unique goals. Decide what jobs you are most interested in as well as what types of jobs you would be willing to accept. Only apply to those positions for which you are willing to accept an offer. This sounds like simple enough advice but some may feel the need to apply more broadly than they are ultimately willing to go. While there's nothing inherently wrong about this, it will waste both your time, a precious commodity during your first year of law school, and that of your interviewers.

Third, only apply for a job at a time when you would be willing to accept an offer for the job. If you would not be willing to accept a job in February, do not apply to that job in February. While many first-year law students may ultimately accept a "second choice" offer, try to stage your applications so that you apply at a time you are willing to accept that offer given the lack of other offers from your first choice employers.

2. Where

There are a wide variety of jobs that will provide you meaningful experience and position you well for second and third year recruiting season. While the availability of these jobs will depend on your specific school and situation, below, I list and discuss certain basic categories.

i. Judge

Most judges provide internships for first-summer law students. At this job, you will perform many of the same duties as a paid law clerk, including researching law for, and even writing, decisions and court orders. Depending on the judge and the judge's clerks, you may become very involved in the various tasks inherent in overseeing the heavy case load that most judges face. You will also have the opportunity to build a positive relationship with the judge, which may lead to future mentoring opportunities and recommendations on your behalf.

If you are interested in a clerkship, government, or litigation position after graduation, an internship with a judge is one of the best ways to spend your first summer; I have even seen experienced attorneys note on their website biography their internship position with a particular judge, although I personally would be reticent to list such a position. Regardless of future interests, a judicial internship looks great on any law student's resume. The only downside is that these positions are unpaid.

You will want to conduct your application process for such a position carefully, as judicial internship positions are generally competitive. The ability to land such an internship will depend on how prestigious and powerful the judge's position is. For example, it will be much more difficult to obtain an internship with a federal judge than a state judge.

Be sure that you are interested in such a position before applying and, if you are, prepare to apply early and move quickly. Judges do not have the recruiting apparatus that law firms possess to coordinate many applicants, and it will be awkward if you turn down an offer. Moreover, many judges are able to receive sufficient applications to fill out their internship programs quickly given the desirability of the job.

ii. Corporate Law Department

Many public corporations, financial firms, and other businesses offer internships to first-year law students. Generally, these positions are paid, although the amount will vary significantly - from minimum wage to a pro-rata portion of a full-time salary. These positions are best for students interested in working at a law firm after graduation and particularly well-suited for students interested in transactional or corporate advisory practice areas.

The timing of these opportunities is somewhat unique. These positions will become available throughout the first year recruiting season but will generally skew later in the spring semester compared to other types of positions available to first-year students. The simple reason is that many internship programs at corporations are revisited annually based on whether the funds, need, and interest are there. As a result, many corporations will only decide to send out recruiting notices late in the spring semester. If you really want such a position, you may have to take the risk of not having a job relatively late in the spring semester. If you are more risk averse, you may want to consider a different path.

These positions will both demand certain qualities in applicants that other positions do not as well as not care about certain qualifications that other positions may require. On one hand, many of these positions will expect applicants to demonstrate some level of interest in their particular field and/or company. An internship or research assistant job is something that any law student would be interested in, and thus interviewers for such positions won't necessary press on why applicants are interested. However, corporations use their internship programs to mentor future attorneys interested in the industry in question, in addition to obtaining relatively inexpensive labor. The salary provided to interns only increases the desire on the part of the corporation to ensure a good fit.

As a result, be sure to thoroughly investigate the company and its industry, and be able to explain at an interview why you are particularly interested in that industry and company. You should be sure to highlight any prior experience in the corporate world, including internships during college or positions between college and law school. In addition, those with a bachelors' degree or a certificate in a business-related field should be sure to mention such qualifications on a cover letter. Another result of the search for "fit" will be that, as opposed to a judicial internship where you may get an offer after a single half-hour interview, at a corporation you may be asked to meet numerous people to ensure that you are a good fit. Still, no one will expect you to be certain that you intend to enter the industry in question upon graduation, so don't feel the need to oversell.

On the other hand, corporations will generally be more relaxed about grades than large law firms or prestigious government or judicial positions. Corporate America is not known for being an extremely intellectual place, and many in-house lawyers are more interested in ensuring that an intern will be a good cultural fit with the office and interested in the work than seeing an "A" in Civil Procedure on a transcript. Another reason for this lack of focus on grades is that first-year law courses have little to do with corporate law, except as background such as with regard to contracts.

iii. Large Law Firm

A summer associate position at a large law firm is generally considered the most difficult job to obtain during one's first summer. There are very few jobs at such firms available to first-year students and most law firms focus the vast majority of their time and energy recruiting second-year students.

This is because law firms run summer associate programs not to mentor students or get additional man-hours but to recruit future full-time employees. It is second year students that will have the potential to receive and accept full-time offers of employment; first year students, on the other hand, will have to come back to the firm the next summer at best, and at worst will simply cash the large checks paid by the law firm during the first summer and then move to another, perhaps, more prestigious, law firm for the second summer and a full-time position. In my experience, very few first-year summer associates returned for their second summer or full-time. Students generally regard such positions as simple cash cows.

This lack of jobs is coupled with the high demand for any such jobs by law students. Law students are highly attracted to such jobs due to the salaries, generally at or close to the level provided to first-year associates on a pro-rata basis, paid to summer associates as well as the significant amount of prestige associated with such positions. Given how hard they are to come by, obtaining a job at a large law firm during one's first summer will position a law student exceptionally well during second-year interviews, although the importance of such a position is, like everything else, easily displaced by grades.

Getting hired as a first-year student will require truly outstanding grades, ample personal interview skills, and many times an additional connection or "X" factor. Good grades will likely not be sufficient here given the reality that even those firms that hire first-year students will limit their hiring to a very small handful of students, even as few as a single student.

Further, given the competition among law students for these positions as well as the lack of need for law firms to extend offers to students at particular schools to maintain relationships, the process is more unstructured than a second-year recruiting. As a result, unless you literally have straight "A"s, extensive networking may be your best opportunity to obtain an interview as a first year. Comprehensively research every connection you may have at a firm and, if your connections like you, have those connections submit your application rather than via HR. See below on the section regarding on-campus interviews for more information on how to interview with large law firms.

In terms of timing, large law firms move the earliest compared to other employers. If you are seriously interested in working at a large law firm, submit applications as early as you can after you receive your fall grades; as mentioned before, it can't hurt to submit immediately after the close of the fall semester, although it is probably not necessary given the focus on grades. In terms of timing for accepting an offer, while firms will permit customary periods for consideration of an offer, if you receive an offer you would be a fool to make them wait too long after the gift just provided you.

iv. Small Law Firm

Much more common than positions at large law firms are positions at small and boutique law firms. For these positions, there is a much more straightforward path to obtain a job and clear goals for the employers for providing them. Forget mentoring, forget industry knowledge, forget recruiting; here is a class of employer that is actually looking to accomplish the shocking goal of getting law students to do work.

While with regard to mid-size firms the way in which you obtain and work at your job will likely be largely equivalent to large law firms, smaller firms may be quite different. Here, the real-world nature of the opportunity set here also means that there will be greater variability in the professionalism involved. In other words, you might be working with, to use a technical legal term here, whack jobs. While large law firms are crazy in their own right, there is an overlay of professionalism and dignity at the vast majority of these firms that those who do not have experience at smaller law firms may not appreciate. Smaller firms and solo practitioners, in particular, may not be able, or willing, to maintain the same level of decorum.

Your stomach for working in such environments will largely depend on how important getting paid is to you. While money is nice, the ultimate prize is obtaining full-time employment, and first-year employment is almost nothing from a financial perspective compared to that. As a result, you may want to think seriously about accepting a judicial internship or other unpaid work that will look quite good on your resume, in fact, probably much better than an unrecognized law firm name.

To be sure, there are also benefits from such a position. There are many small and mid-size law firms in every legal market. At such a job you will likely get on-the-ground practical experience in the area(s) of law in which the law firm practices. You may be involved in a wide variety of tasks and, given the relatively close proximity you will have to the attorneys, it will likely be an eye-opening experience and you will hopefully learn a great deal. You will likely be able to glean several noteworthy stories for use in second and third-year interviews, and you also may receive a mentor in the process. Ultimately, your experience may not be worse than at other positions, and it may even be better, but it certainly will be more uncertain.

v. Public Service Organization

Many law students work at public service organizations during the summer after their first year of law school, and with good reason. At these organizations, students can get unbeatable front-line experience assisting the full-time attorneys on their heavy case load, all the while making a difference in the lives of underprivileged individuals in an authentic way.

There are a wide variety of public service organizations with needs for law student interns. Many of these organizations, such as The Legal Aid Society, provide legal representation to individuals who cannot afford to pay a lawyer. Such organizations represent clients in housing disputes, family law, and general civil cases, primarily in disputes or other interaction with local, state or federal government agencies.

Working for such an organization may be an excellent way to spend a summer. While working as an associate, I worked on a pro bono basis with several of these organizations and was successful in helping several disadvantaged people. Such work is both professionally and personally rewarding, and during your first summer you will have an opportunity to immerse in such work for an extended amount of time before the reality of full-time work sets in. In addition, the significant substantive legal responsibility you will likely be provided at these understaffed agencies will be helpful in interviews, and many law schools provide stipends for those students who work at such agencies over a summer.

These organizations will also look to ensure that successful applicants share an interest in their mission. Therefore, research the organization, market any relevant work experience, and, in general, clearly indicate why you are interested in working in public service. Like with corporations, there is no need, however, to pretend that you are intent on entering public service full-time if you are not. These organizations know the drill and are appreciative of the free help, but like to partner with sympathetic voices. This is especially so since many public service attorneys have a conflicted view of attorneys that work in the private sector - as both "sell outs" and essential elements of serving their clients via pro bono representation.

Despite the lack of pay, positions at public service organizations are in high demand due to the high quality of the work and experience. If you are interested in public service, be sure to apply relatively early in the spring semester, both to those organizations that are actively seeking applicants from your law school as well as reaching out to a wide spectrum of similar organizations in your area. Like with a judge, only apply if you are interested in accepting and be prepared to accept offers soon after they are provided to you, as these organizations do not have patience or infrastructure for a comprehensive recruiting program.

vi. Professor

Speaking of free help, no one is more excited to accept it than law school professors. Professors are expected to publish extensively in law reviews and other venues. To publish any serious work of legal scholarship requires extensive research, a skill that many law students are looking to improve. As a result, many law professors hire first-summer law students as research assistants. If all goes well and both sides are interested, the job may continue part-time during the academic year as well.

Working as a research assistant can provide several benefits. It is a well-trodden path for law students and will be respected by interviewers. It will certainly provide you with improvements in your research skills. More importantly, it will provide you with exposure to and hopefully a relationship with a law professor. As discussed previously, such a relationship can be invaluable for a variety of reasons. Most practically, if your professor is particularly prominent, your second-year interviewers will be interested in learning about your experience with the professor and the position will serve as an asset in interviews.

Obtaining a research assistant position is one of the more straightforward employment processes available to first-year students. Professors will advertise the vast majority of these positions publicly via the schools' standard communication channels to students, such as the school's career services website. Positions working for prominent faculty members are highly in demand and, therefore, quite competitive, but if you are interested and diligent, you should be able to nab a position with some professor at the school.

Of course, as mentioned before, the best way to get such positions with the professors that teach your first-year courses is to commence a relationship with the professor far in advance of when the position becomes available. Like with other positions not provided by large organizations, be sure to only apply if interested and be ready to accept if offered. It will be particularly awkward if you decline an offer provided (in person, traditionally) by a law school faculty member, particularly those with which you have or may in the future take classes.

vii. Government Agency

Another excellent option for spending your first summer is working as a legal intern at a federal, state or local government agency. While impossible to overly generalize about the experience provided by such a wide variety of organizations, such internships are generally very much appreciated by law students as they look great on a resume, provide an inside look at the workings of these agencies, may at times feature high-profile or otherwise noteworthy work prime for use in future interview discussions, and may even lead to future employment.

The formality attached to the process will depend on what type of agency is involved. Federal agencies will publicize their openings. Internships at federal agencies are highly competitive, approaching the level of difficulty of obtaining a job at a large law firm, and will be generally provided to students with excellent grades and otherwise possessing a history of a high level of academic achievement. The applications for such positions are formal and written with strict deadlines relatively early in the recruiting season. By contrast, local and some state agencies may have a relatively less formal process and be willing to accept students with mediocre grades.

4. How to Get a First Year Job

It is easy to talk about the advantages of different types of jobs when you don't need one. More difficult and important is how to find out about these jobs. Below I discuss just that - some pieces of advice to apply to the first year job hunt in addition to the general advice regarding legal job hunting I provide below in the context of second year interviews.

The first thing to realize about the first year job hunt is that you are largely on your own. While many top law schools provide extensive on-campus interviewing during the second year, during the first year you will have to hit "send" or "submit," and ask a firm to interview you rather than receive such opportunities automatically. As a result, especially if you are intent on a paying or otherwise competitive job, you may have to devote a significant amount of time to apply for these jobs (another reason why it is a bad idea to start during the fall semester). You may need to send out hundreds of resumes and engage in numerous interviews during the first year to get exactly what you wanted - a laborious process indeed. You will have to decide whether such efforts are worth the loss of studying time.

The first step is to decide what type of job you are interested in and avoid applying to those jobs you would refuse if offered. Be realistic about the types of opportunities available to you. Working at a large law firm during a first summer will largely only be available to students at the top law schools and only for those students that have excellent grades. Applying to a lot of large law firms will take a lot of time, and barring a truly robust personal connection, which can open up almost any door, you may decide based on your situation that applying to such firms is a waste of your time.

Once you do settle on a category or categories of positions in which you are interested, be comprehensive about the sources you use to obtain interviews. To start, personal connections are a truly robust way to obtain interviews. Think carefully about who you know - working for any of the types of organizations listed above - that may work for an employer that could use legal help. In addition to friends, friends of your family, and business contacts from your life before law school, consider a broad range of your acquaintances. Especially if you are not seeking to be paid, be optimistic about the readiness of loose connections to be willing to help out. Many employers look fondly at their employees referring them applicants for jobs or even internships, so your connections may want to help from a selfish perspective as well.

In terms of more formal channels of finding positions, first, explore every publicly posted position. Read your school's career services job board religiously, as well as other online sources. In addition to jobs currently advertised on a job board, research jobs that prior law students from the law school obtained, as the employer may not have advertised yet but is intending on hiring students.

Further, if you are intent on a particular type of job, develop a fairly comprehensive set of potential employers for such jobs in the geographic area you are targeting. While in some areas, such as New York City, developing a truly comprehensive list will be impossible, the more you apply the better your chances of getting a taker. Identify the firms, pick someone on their website that seems like a decision-maker, and send a relatively short cover letter email and resume. There may be nothing particularly noteworthy about your grades or your background, but if the employer has a need for legal help, having your resume in hand without competition from a hundred others will in many cases put you ahead of the pack for any opportunity. The one caveat is that you should not be expected to get paid for positions that are unadvertised.

Above all, if you want to be aggressive either during the first-year search or during the second or third year, you cannot be discouraged by several or even tens or hundreds of "Nos". You are competing against thousands of other equally, if not more, qualified candidates and you must be extremely persistent if you want to succeed.

While your career services office may likely be of some help in your effort, do not rely on them. Similar to what this book discussed with regard to pre-law advisors, career services personnel work for the university and not for you personally. They are ultimately attempting to ensure the career placement of all of the school's students generally and not your best interests; this is not at all an indictment, just hopefully a statement of the obvious.

This means that you have to know what would be the best fit in terms of first-year employment for you and seek out such opportunities as they become available. Additionally, you should seek feedback on your resume, interview style, and strategy from others who may be more frank with you about your deficiencies than career services staff. It may be that a certain position is not advertised to first-year students, but you may want to apply anyway in the event you have other qualifications making you an ideal candidate. It may be that you believe it is best for you to continue your search far into the spring semester or alternatively to accept an offer early. Ultimately, simply remember that career services staff are not your spouse or your parents.

5. Conclusion

Your ultimate goal should be to find a position that fulfills three criteria. First, an employer that is recognized or unwilling to accept just anyone - i.e. not a divorce lawyer in a storefront and not your dad or mom. Second, a position that is relatively interesting or financially rewarding. Third, job duties that provide some interesting tidbits for use in your second-year interviews. As a large percentage of legal employers should be able to fulfill all three criteria, above all don't overly worry about your first-year employment.

C. Other Uses of First Summer

There are two other opportunities during a first summer - informational interviews to meet more experienced lawyers without seeking a job and attending cocktail receptions provided by law firms hoping to recruit students. As explained below, consider the former more than the latter.

An Informational interview is where a student or other interested party meets a professional to ask them questions about their job and company and discuss their own background while making clear that the student is not seeking a job from the professional. Such interviews may be worth an investment of your time, either during your first summer or during your second or third year of law school. In my view, the more advice you get and the more sources it comes from, the better advised you will be in making the choice best for you. These interviews are also practically helpful in a variety of ways depending on your situation. Certainly, these interviews will be an excellent preparation for the important interviews coming the next year.

These contacts benefit a wide variety of students. If you are at a prestigious school and are interested in and confident in your ability to obtain an entry-level job at a large law firm, such interviews will also permit you, without the overlay of self-interest from actually interviewing, to meet attorneys at mid-size and corporate employers that you may be interested in after a few years at the law firm. For students who are less certain, these interviews will provide you with contacts in the legal world as you navigate trying to secure an entry-level position during your second and third year of law school.

Reach out and don't be shy about "taking up people's time." In my experience, many lawyers are thrilled, even honored, at the potential to provide people advice. Think about it - this person may be slaving away day and night for ungrateful bosses and doing largely uninteresting work. You are offering him or her a welcome distraction from all that in order to unambiguously help another human being while being consulted as an expert and benefactor of knowledge. As those friends of yours who decided to go to business school would say, it's a win win.

On the other hand, the cocktail receptions, while harmless, are largely a waste of time. These events are a somewhat bizarre dance where the law firms are only holding them to attract law students, the lawyers attending the events are only doing so to satisfy their employers and law students are only going to help their chances of obtaining a job with the law firm. In other words, no one actually wants to be there, and as a result, these events tend to have a poor atmosphere. While there is the off chance that you will actually strike a chord with a decision maker that will improve your chances, such events largely end the same way they began - with everyone wanting to go somewhere else and get on with their lives. There is very little chance that anyone will remember you for the better, while if you say or do anything stupid - a potentiality that the copious amount of alcohol available at such events tends to make possible - there is the very good chance you will be remembered in a way that you wished you weren't. Go if you must, but building personal connections in venues where you can more credibly show interest in a lawyer's career is probably where you will get the greatest return.

Chapter 7: Getting a Job

This chapter is probably the most important in this book. While getting good grades during the first year of law school is essential as a prerequisite to a successful beginning to a legal career, those grades are only the means to the ultimate end of gaining full-time entry-level legal employment.

This chapter will help you navigate this process. It will first discuss how to research law firms and determine who to request interviews with, then discuss how to prepare a resume and in general prepare yourself for the interview process, and finally provide tips on the actual interviews. It then distinguishes between the process of on campus interviewing (known as "OCI") for summer associate positions for those law students who are fortunate to receive such interviews and the process of seeking entry-level employment outside of OCI, and discusses various approaches to obtain a full-time position outside of OCI.

A. Researching Law Firms

The prospect of researching prospective employers is a new issue for many, if not most law school students, with perhaps the exception of those who previously worked in finance. Many will have spent their entire prior life in school with only summer internships or other part-time jobs. Even for those with a couple of years of work experience, they may have gained such jobs in a relatively straightforward manner without having to engage in significant market research. To make matters worse, law schools provide little to no training or other support for engaging in such research.

Whether or not it is a familiar task, relatively comprehensive legal market research is an important step for every law student to take given the numerous potential paths for the transition from student to employee. Law is a very decentralized industry, perhaps because it is relatively unregulated, with many mid-size and large firms and numerous boutiques in even the smallest practice areas and geographic markets. While there have been many law firm mergers in recent years, law is different from industries such as consulting, investment banking or public accounting in the sheer diversity of entry-level options available that would look great on a resume. You can only know what options are out there and have insight into what would be the best fit for you if you make the effort to learn about the industry.

In terms of timing, you should start researching as early as possible. Preferably, the latest time to do so is during your first summer. You should provide yourself with enough time prior to the beginning of interviews to allow you engage in comprehensive research - i.e. don't wait until the week before interviews begin. Given that you won't need such research to get through an initial screening interview, and you will only be granted a call-back interview at a relatively small subset of the firms you are researching, you may be tempted to simply push off researching firms until you know which are still in play after your initial screens. However, there simply won't be enough time to research the firms you are considering during the call-back period.

1. Set Criteria

The first step in the research process is arriving at your relevant universe of firms outside of which you are not interested. This is a subjective determination and will depend on what qualifications you insist on in a legal employer. For those who are planning, at least initially, to gain a job through on-campus interviewing, the universe may simply be those firms that are coming to your school's event. For many, geography will be a limiting factor, either because one is insistent on remaining in a particular geographic area or because the law school in question largely places students only in a particular area.

2. What Sources to Obtain

i. Public Information

The next step is to read publicly available material about these firms. At least with regard to large and larger mid-size firms, there is a variety of information available on the Web. One of the best ways to learn substantive information about the work the firm does is via Chambers & Partners, which provides helpful rankings and information on the top performers in a variety of practice areas, based on feedback and reviews from actual clients. The NALP Directory provides basic information such as salaries, the number of lawyers practicing at each firm, and those that identify themselves as members of minority groups. Further, while areas of the firm website such as the recruiting page will be generic, other information on a firm web site may be highly revealing. If the firm's press releases are dominated by announcements of lateral partner additions, that may shed helpful light on your partnership prospects at the firm. Announcements of litigations won and deals closed will also help you understand where the firm's strengths lie, and news stories may also be revealing. Finally, while this method of research may sound a bit juvenile, researching comments in online forums or even connecting with current or former associates in such forums can be an important source of current information on firms, even if discounted to reflect the likely negatively self-selecting nature of who would volunteer information in such venues.

Based on this information, you should be able to determine which firms have a practice area in your area of interest within your geographic location or other limitations. If you are absolutely gung-ho on working as an ERISA lawyer in New York City and have the luxury of insisting on such limitations, there is no point speaking with firms without a practice group there. For practice area, even the size of the practice is highly relevant information - a practice group of 50 attorneys is much more likely to need additional junior associate help and have partnership opportunities than a practice group of three attorneys.

There are also several publicly available resources purporting to provide more candid information on life at relatively large firms from associates. Chambers Associate provides law firm information, such as statements on law firm culture, provided by associates in a format designed for law students. The Vault company also provides such information in books and subscription-based websites. Unfortunately, the information provided by these sites is relatively unhelpful, as associate reviewers appear to be self-selecting in generally only submitting relatively positive reviews. By way of example, even for those firms which are widely acknowledged as having cut-throat pressure cooker-like cultures, these guides include relatively passé or even glowing reviews.

ii. Private Information

The more helpful research on firms, large and small, will come from more localized if unscientific research with individuals. While you obviously won't have nearly the time, resources or interest in doing this kind of research for a wide variety of firms, for those firms in which you are particularly interested you should seek out former summer associates or former associates and ask them about their experiences at the firm. The best place to do so is, of course, at your law school, where there may be several third-year students who worked at the firm the prior summer. The law school should also have lists of alumni that you can mine for this purpose. You should also examine your friends and contacts to see if you can identify leads through your network.

If those methods don't produce hits, you may consider using LinkedIn to identify leads. The service, especially if you subscribe to one of the premium versions, includes robust searching capabilities that might help you identify former associates. While the best way to connect with these people would be to identify mutual connections, some of the people you reach out to through LinkedIn may be willing to speak with you as a courtesy.

The one exception where such individualized research is not likely to be helpful, and even potentially hurtful, is if you reach out to current employees. While alumni of your school may be helpful to provide general career advice or informational interviews, the vast majority will not be willing to discuss their current firm in any type of candor. This is many times true even if you are friends with the person in question, as, understandably, associates care about their own career first and many associates worry about any negative comment getting back to those in positions of power at the firm. Indeed, you should expect that many associates will report to the recruiting department or others at the law firm that you reached out to them.

However, while affirmatively reaching out to current associates is not likely to be effective, you should definitely take seriously any feedback, explicit or implicit, that such employees provide during the interview process. Associates will usually be unflappable advocates of their firm, but may at times provide revealing answers about the firm or its partners, at times openly and at times in coded language or cues.

3. Information to Seek

What aspects of law firms should you be researching and inquiring about? Typically, many public materials, as well as many law students, focus on generic and generalized issues such as what type of work is available to associates, what the firm culture is like, what the hours and compensation look like, availability of pro bono and diversity programs, and generalized firm strategy. The problem with such issues is that the responses sound the same for almost every firm and individuals may not have good or even accurate answers to these questions. In the public materials, every firm supports pro bono (as, truly, most of them do), every firm has tough hours but a "collegial" culture where "associates feel free to stop by a partner's office to ask a question." Wow - communication can be in-person in addition to telephonically and written? Say no more. Sounds like the place for me!

Instead of such generalized inquiries revealing pat answers, look to ask specific questions. What is the firm's typical road map for associate development - are associates quickly expected to produce or ship out, or are they given extended development time frames? Similarly, what is the firm's outlook for promoting partners from within - a rare occurrence with most appointments coming from lateral partners, or yearly and almost mandatory?

It's also a good idea to seek information on the various practice areas of the firm, including the practice area of the person you are speaking to and any practice areas in which you are interested. Does the practice area have its own clients, or does it service the clients brought to the firm by lawyers in another practice area? What kind of work does it do - what kind of transactions or litigations, and for which type of clients?

A third productive avenue of inquiry are questions regarding the lived experiences of actual people, which you can hopefully receive by speaking to former summer associates or former associates. What was that individual's experience interacting with partners, and what were the experiences of his or her acquaintances at the firm? Are associates expected to find their own work (what is known as a "free market" system)? What happens if an associate stops doing work for a particular partner or group of partners - will he or she be able to receive work from others at the firm? Is the firm open to allowing associates to switch practice areas?

Such personalized questions may provide revealing anecdotes and a greater willingness to share than more generic inquiries. In addition, mentioning that you are acquaintances with the former summer associates you speak to in making such inquiries makes you look good in an interview as it broadcasts that you have a particular interest in the firm and that you fit in with the type of people who work as summer associates at the firm.

In particular, determining the unique aspects of each firm's culture is important. Most large firms are slightly different than every other firm in certain ways, and determining what each firm's culture is like is important to your getting a job, given that people prefer similar people to themselves, and to your succeeding in such a job given the amount of time you will be spending at work, and the expectation to fit in that will be present at every firm.

While some of you may be sneering at the need to think carefully about culture, not caring about a firm's culture is sort of like not caring about the personality of a potential spouse and only caring about their looks, intelligence, earning potential, and parenting ability. Working relationships, especially those involving very high salaries and important work for important clients, are just like any other relationship that needs a connection, a good fit, to be successful. Even if you don't intend to stick around at a law firm permanently (i.e. almost everyone), this is a serious job that you will be expected to be seriously committed to, and the better the fit the easier that will be.

It's also important to analyze culture based on fit specifically and not "good" or "bad." When some law students speak about culture, they focus on avoiding high-intensity firms where there are partners who are aggressive "screamers." To this telling, such firms are "bad" and the ones where these type of people are not welcome are the "good" firms. At "good" firms, partner and associate compensation is lockstep based on seniority, while at the "bad" firms, partners get paid based on how much business they bring in, what is known as "eat what you kill," and associate compensation is individualized.

The reality is that all law firms are crazy in their own right. The fundamental nature of law firms is crazy - old people making money purportedly based on their delivery of highly complex legal advice to sophisticated business clients while in reality based on how much they can overwork young people. As the very nature of law firm life is crazy, there will be craziness in every single law firm. No exceptions.

However, that craziness will be different in different firms. At some firms, the culture will skew aggressive, where partners may loosen their vocal cords a bit when upset but may be equally ebullient about your good work. Partners at more aggressive firms may compete for how to divide up firm revenues, but that focus on business development on the part of all partners (at least those that want to make money) may provide opportunities for young associates to get involved in business development projects, which can provide client contact and sharpen a variety of useful skills for the associate.

At the firms that skew passive aggressive, partners may not scream at you, but they may go to the other extreme on the feedback spectrum and smile at you the entire year only to tell you at your review that you are going to be fired. They may make cutting snide remarks about you in front of others that sting far worse than a few loud words, or ignore your contributions as much as they do your mistakes. Not better or worse - just different.

Some students indeed may not fit with an aggressive culture. But others will, in the same way that some people prefer that their friends and spouses skew aggressive and upfront rather than needy and passive aggressive. And of course, most firms that don't fit neatly into one of two simple boxes of "aggressive" and "passive aggressive" - every firm is slightly different. The goal while you still haven't committed is to figure out, to the extent you have the luxury of making choices about these things, where you fit the best.

B. Interviews

There is, perhaps, no aspect of the entire process of becoming a lawyer that is more naturally fraught with tension than the entry-level interview. Despite your years of hard work and endless late nights in the library, your fate is ultimately determined in the course of a twenty-minute meeting with someone you have never met and who may be alternatively extremely important or extremely junior at the firm in question. Might your interviewer have just received an upsetting or stress-inducing text from their spouse or significant other, or a nasty email from someone at work or a client? For sure. Your interview scheduled right before lunch on a day your interviewer didn't have breakfast? Definitely possible. Any chance that interviewers will compensate in their evaluation for their realization that these or myriad other factors completely beyond your control affected their judgment? Nada.

Despite these seemingly foreboding issues, the reality is that entry-level law firm interviews are not that substantively challenging when compared to other industries and interviewing for future jobs. This is true most fundamentally in terms of the structure of the interview process. In the legal industry, there is only a two-step interview process for even the most elite firms. In this process, first, you undergo an initial screening interview with generally one person and lasting at most 30 minutes. Next, you undergo "call-back" interviews (i.e. that you engage in because you were "called back" to the firm after your initial screening) with 3-6 people that can take from a couple of hours to close to an entire day in a couple of instances.

That's it, except from, perhaps, a business lunch as part of the call-back process. In other industries, you may have to undergo such steps as a battery of tests to measure fundamental aspects of yourself or your relevant skills, engaging in up to 8 rounds of interviews with almost the entire team that you might be working with, and/ or engaging in joint exercises with other interviewees. Indeed, even within the legal industry, many applicants for jobs requiring experience, as opposed to entry-level associate positions, must undergo such grueling steps.

Moreover, the differences are just as stark when the substance of the questions asked at law firm interviews is compared to other industries. Law firm partners and associates will generally exclusively stick to traditional interview questions, eschewing the numerous difficult questions that abound in interviews for positions at consulting and investment banking firms, as well as other industries.

First, interviews will universally begin with a generalized request to "tell me about yourself" in which you should provide a thoughtful but relatively concise summary of the following:

- why you are interested in law

- why you are interested in the firm's summer associate program in particular, and

- why your background will be an asset to you.

While this sounds somewhat similar to a law school personal statement, the difference is that with a law firm your thoughts should be a lot more commercial - talk about your interest in being a business advisor, not in saving the world.

Second, the interviewer will ask you a series of fairly standard interview questions regarding your resume and your future interests. Your goal throughout this stage should be to tie each answer back to the three points of interest above.

Finally, with about five minutes to spare, the interviewer will typically ask you if you have any questions about the law firm. You should have at least three questions pre-packaged for each interview. You should ask questions that indicate a familiarity with the firm in question that could not have been asked of any firm, although there is no need to be esoteric. To the extent you can ask questions that the interviewer him or herself, based on his or her practice area and level of seniority, would have a personal interest in or knowledge of, that will help you gain a personal connection to the interviewer.

Given the straight-forward nature of law firm interviews, it behooves you to ensure that you put your best foot forward, as missteps will not be forgiven. To prepare you for interviews, I have compiled a list of "dos" that you should ensure you follow as well as a list of "don'ts" that you should definitely avoid.

DO

Mock interview extensively. Work with whoever is willing to work with you before interview season and prepare stock answers to many of the most typical questions (lists of which should be available from your law school).

These interviews are anything but natural, and it may take you time to get used to how unnatural they are. Of course, the need to practice goes only to a point; don't sound rehearsed, just practice enough to be rehearsed without sounding like it.

Respect all of the traditional trappings of an interview. Treat each OCI interview as if each were an individually scheduled meeting and not just the artificial process of running in and out of hotel rooms. Even if the courtesy is not returned, it will make a favorable impression. Want to start the conversation yourself since you know what the first question will be? Too bad. When you become managing partner of a large law firm you can change the way the firm interviews people, not now.

Include some hobbies or other interests, assuming they are relatively common, on a line in your resume. Sports aficionado? Gourmet cooking expert? Global gallivanter? Awesome. World record holder for the number of bees held in a beard? Maybe not.

Appear relatively relaxed, friendly, and affable. By far, the most important aspect of an entry-level law firm interview is that the interviewer subjectively likes you as a human being. Purportedly, the reason is so that they know you will not be a pain to work with given the frequently grueling nature associated with law firm work. Whether or not there is any substantive reason for it, people ultimately want to favor people they like, and that is especially true in "law firm land" where there is little substance to the interview. Make relatively light banter and laugh when your interviewer laughs.

Show flexibility and a can-do attitude. Most projects at law firms are on teams, and associates need to be "team players," willing to work closely together with a wide variety of other people and step up to do whatever is necessary. Having annoying people on the team is a painful experience for everyone and law firms try very hard to weed oppositional personalities out.

Wear a conservative suit. Men should wear a conservative, two-button solid navy or charcoal suit with tie and black shoes and women should wear an equivalently conservative business suit. However, there is absolutely no need to purchase an expensive suit. It will not help you and many lawyers will be too tired to even notice. Law students are not expected to be wealthy enough to afford expensive clothing.

Articulate a basic interest in a practice area that the firm likely needs help with. Many interviewers want to see that law students have devoted at least some thought to what they want to do with the rest of their lives, given the specialized nature of most complex legal work.

Sound interested in the firm, what the interviewer is saying, and the interviewer's work. Have zero interest in litigation, or securitization, or whatever it is the interviewer is doing? There's no expectation that you need to lie and say you want to enter that practice area, which would also perhaps sound disingenuous, but remain interested and open.

Name-drop it like it's hot. While explicit name dropping could very well backfire and probably won't help, it may help to weave into the conversation an indication that you are comfortable and have connections in the corporate and financial world and would potentially be an asset in business development down the line. As noted above, while perhaps it's not fair that people with such connections get ahead, they still do. Use it or lose it.

Grin and bear it. Your interviewers may say the darndest, perhaps even illegal, things. You can take the abuse and potentially get an offer, or indicate disapproval and the interviewer will find another reason to reject your candidacy. I urge you to keep your head down, which is advice that applies generally to your career in addition to interviewing. You owe it to yourself to keep your options open. In addition, at firms that are of the size that they are willing to engage in large scale interviewing at OCI, there is no reason to be sure that the broader firm culture reflects the miscues of a particular interviewer.

Feel free to take a few seconds to think and organize your answer before responding to a question. Don't look like a deer in the headlights for a full minute, of course, but no one expects you to engage in a speed-speaking contest. An articulate, likable answer is what they want.

Treat everyone with respect, including secretaries. This is a general interview tip and hopefully goes without saying, but you never know. In particular, be very careful around recruiting staff. In addition to simply treating them with courtesy, which hopefully you extend to every human being, you should always be "on" around them in a fashion similar to how you act in an interview. These individuals can be very judgmental in a manner that can be difficult to detect but could be significantly averse to your candidacy. Some of these individuals are very close to the firm's partners, including senior management, and you should be very careful around them even if they act casual. In-firm recruiters are not your advocates or your buddies.

DON'T

Indicate a dead-set interest in a very small practice area of that firm, unless you know that the firm is seriously seeking associates to work in that area. Law firms want to know that their associates are flexible, given that hiring needs may change. This advice is especially so for practice areas, such as entertainment law, that require very few associates.

Stand out. An interview is not the place to show you are unique, rebellious, quirky, or anything other than a smart person who is easy to get along with. The law firm website says they welcome a wide variety of personalities? They're lying. They allow flip-flops in the office? Dude, that's after you get the offer. First, you have to make sure you don't end up wearing flip-flops to your basement "office." For whatever reason, law is a profession and an industry that embraces conformity and standardization. Violate the norms at your risk.

Indicate that you are ideologically inflexible. Law firms may, perhaps legitimately, worry that those who express strongly held opinions on political, social or economic issues, especially in an environment as uncomfortable as a law firm interview, will not be flexible enough to take on any legal issue presented by their clients.

Try to sound like you are an expert. You should not try to come off as an expert in any area of the law, in finance, or basically just about anything in which practicing lawyers are expected to be facile. You're not expected to be, and some interviewers might become competitive or simply see your statements as an attempt to overcompensate for insecurity.

Talk too much either for any particular answer or in elongating the interview in general. Keep your answers relatively straightforward and to the point. At the end, ask two to three questions to the interviewer - not six.

Say anything negative about anybody or anything. All of your experiences were excellent, the people you worked with were universally great mentors, and you somehow have an equally solid opinion of large corporations and financial institutions and the prosecutors suing them that you spent your last summer interning with.

Imply you have a clear or authoritative opinion of the firm and its business. By all means, you should research the firm, know what it does and be conversant in recent news related to it, but implying at an early stage that you are focused on one particular firm will sound creepy, disingenuous and /or silly. Of course, at the call-back stage, you will be expected to know a significant amount about the firm, but still based on the understanding that your knowledge and views are still forming, even if you have been stalking the firm since you began law school and know the name of every managing partner since the firm's founding.

Try to play up any abnormal parts of your resume. Don't affirmatively bring up anything that is abnormal, and if the interviewer brings them up, find a skill that you gained from that experience and quickly relate it to the more standard aspects of your resume and your general narrative.

Stretch and try to make your answers more interesting and thoughtful than they have to be. You don't have to be a genius to get this job; you just have to be articulate and indicative of having a good personality. Straightforward, relatively short answers are always better received than a rambling or convoluted attempt to sound smart. Similarly, feel free to ask the same types of standard questions that everyone else does. You will not get more "points" for asking a complex question but will suffer if your attempt makes you look foolish because you got something wrong or what you said makes no sense.

Email (or, heaven forfend, snail mail) thank you letters to your interviewers. As a leading recruiter has articulated,[20] there is much more downside than upside to this maneuver. However, many people continue to think it is a good idea. Perhaps outside of the legal industry, but lawyers are much too critical and busy to appreciate such things.

C. Unique Issues with OCI Process

Perhaps, the most bizarre thing about on-campus interviews is the very fact that many students approach them uncomfortably with nervousness and timidity, instead of with joy or even temerity. Dude, not only do you have an interview for a job paying a ton of money, but you have 20 of them, and they are so excited to meet you that they are coming to your school instead of you having to go to them! OCI, as on-campus interviews are known at many schools, is an incredible privilege and gift you should be grateful for. Well, grateful enough, although to be fair, yes, you are paying $200K + for this privilege. But the point is, you need not be a fearful, huddling law student; rather, you should approach OCI with the excitement and confidence deriving from the realization that they are coming to you, and not the other way around. That being said, like with everything else, don't appear cocky, as that will backfire with many interviewers but especially those who went to less prestigious law schools than you.

Given this dynamic, students approaching OCI need to think about being selective in a couple of ways.

---

[20] http://www.bcgsearch.com/article/60742/Thank-you-letters-risks-vs-benefits/.

The first is in terms of deciding which firms to interview with.[21] In compiling your list, I would urge you to interview with several of the most prestigious firms that you have a shot at getting a job at. Marketplace participants frequently view working at a large law firm as an entry-level associate, and certainly as a summer associate, similar to how they view law school - as a credential. Just as with law school, the more impressive your credential in this area, the more plentiful and interesting your opportunity set, in any legal field, will be in the future, all else being equal. If anything, there is even more reason to value prestige when selecting a law firm to work at than with law schools, as the counterweight of potential scholarship funds that lower-tier law schools may offer does not exist with law firms. Quite the opposite. With the exception of a few boutiques that pay above-market compensation to lure associates, the more prestigious the firm, the more compensation you are likely to make, although many firms near the top of the market will pay roughly the same.

There are, of course, several other factors that you should consider in compiling your list. The list will depend on the unique situation you face. You should select a mix of firms, including some firms that are likely to pass on you based on your grades, some that you are perfectly qualified for, and some safety firms to fall back on if you do unexpectedly poorly in interviews. Thus, your ultimate list will depend on numerous factors specific to your situation, including your school, your grades, and how tight the recruiting market is for entry-level associates.

One other factor to consider is your geographic preferences or limitations. This book discussed considerations for those looking to work outside the geography of the law school when deciding which school to attend. At this stage where you are deciding where to interview, the point made about working harder if you are looking to work outside of the geography of the law school should be made again. If you are serious about that decision, you need to, regardless of your academic record, supplement your OCI with

---

[21] This applies to those schools that allow students to select which firms they wish to interview with. Some schools do have OCI but give the law firms the decision-making power in terms of who to interview.

personally reaching out to other firms in the area that are not interviewing at your school. In addition, as noted above, at some point you will need to make a decision on whether to go ahead with starting a career in the law school's geography or insisting on the geography you had planned on; certainly, it will be more difficult to switch geographies later on.

One final factor to consider is what practice areas you are particularly interested in, if you have such preferences. As a basic example, you should not interview with Quinn Emanuel, a prominent litigation-focused firm, if you have no interest in litigation. If you are focused on a particularly small niche, such as entertainment law, unless you truly have stratospheric grades, be sure to supplement the firms that have that niche with well-known firms that have general corporate and litigation practices. The reality is that many people interested in such niches do not get offers to join these small practice groups.

Finally, one factor that I would countervailingly urge you to lessen your consideration of, although perhaps not completely eliminate, are certain claims about law firm life. Many law firms make, almost verbatim, similar claims about how working at their firm will be a good experience, including that their firm provides "early responsibility" to associates and that their firm is particularly supportive of pro bono, diversity, or similar programs outside of billable work.

In terms of pro bono, essentially every large law firm in New York City strongly supports their associates' efforts at pro bono, and of course numerous firms across the country also do so. To be fair, there are some firms that outshine others in terms of the importance of the cases they take on, but if you are looking simply for opportunities to give back and gain practical experience from pro bono matters, that is something available at almost every large law firm.

It will be equally difficult to judge firms based on the purported level of experience they provide associates. While many law students may instinctively think that lower-prestige firms may offer better experiences, this is a dubious claim and not worth the loss of credential value that higher-prestige firms provide. I received a very good set of experience from the high-prestige firms I worked at, and I believe many similarly situated associates at other firms would agree. If anything, higher-prestige firms at times may provide better experience to junior associates, as they will simply have so much work that senior personnel are not able to handle it all, while senior personnel at lower-prestige firms may horde the few opportunities of substantive experience that come their way. In addition, whatever type of firm you work at, generally, associates held in high regard will be provided exposure to good opportunities. It may be that at truly small firms, new associates receive more substantive experience than those at large or mid-size firms, but these firms pay only a fraction of what large law firms pay and your opportunity set will dramatically diminish if you take a job at such a firm.

D. Getting a Job Outside of a Summer Associate Program

While some law students obtain a job at a summer associate program and a full-time offer afterwards most law students do not. While the inability to obtain such an opportunity may be initially disappointing, such students can take comfort in that obtaining an entry-level job is very much in your hands. Jobs will go to those who push the most, hustle the hardest, and pound the most pavement, and you can obtain one even if you don't have the best grades, assuming they are at least average. This section discusses the differences between the OCI and non-OCI recruiting processes and provides thoughts on how to go about locating job opportunities.

i. Distinctions Between OCI and Everyone Else

One major difference is the **lack of standardization of interviews.** Every firm and employer will be slightly different in their recruiting system and how they substantively conduct the interviews. Indeed, as a result of the lack of standardization in this context, it is difficult for me to provide specific advice. Some interviewers may be more aggressive in pursuing questioning and focus more closely on whether your experience is relevant to the position. At some firms, you will meet several people in the first round, rather than an initial screening round with a single person. Some firms will ask for actual work product, such as a writing sample. Finally, it may be even more important at firms outside OCI to flatter the interviewer, as organizations other than large law firms will have different systems for determining who advances, there may be no "recruiting committee" like at large law firms and the interviewer may consider him or herself largely free to make a purely discretionary decision. Finally, while large non-law firm organizations will still want you to give a convincing case why their organization is different, small and even some mid-size law firms may not see this as essential as they may not have the arrogance that many large law firms do in purporting that they have a unique culture and experience.

A second difference is the **time frame**. While the OCI process standardizes time frame for interviewing, accepting offers for summer associate programs and accepting offers to rejoin a firm full-time, the time frame for getting a job outside of OCI is completely open. Many law students left out of OCI will take an internship during the summer between the second and third year of law school that is similar to the internships all students engage in during the first summer. Even for those who obtain an internship at a law firm, many of the firms that hire outside of OCI will not necessarily extend full-time offers to any of their summer interns. Thus, many students may find themselves interviewing throughout much of their third year of law school, and even after graduation. Others will secure a summer associateship at a mid-size or relatively small firm outside of OCI from which they will secure a full-time offer to return to the firm after graduation.

This open time frame increases the importance of maintaining a solid GPA during the second and third year of law school, and may generally result in increased anxiety for students in this situation as compared to their OCI cousins. Ultimately, the time frame for obtaining a full-time position is not necessarily later, but simply more variable - you have to be prepared to receive an offer very quickly just as much as you have to be prepared to not receive one until six months after you graduate.

The third difference is the **increased need to determine which field of law one wants to enter**. As opposed to many large law firms who interview at OCI, many small and mid-size law firms practice in only a few specialized fields and/or have clients in only a few industries. Law students in this situation will need to understand these different fields, consider their own strengths and interests, and make a commitment, via accepting a job offer, to a particular practice area and type of employer. This is required even if it is theoretically possible to apply for every legal job of any type in the geographic area in question, because employers in such limited fields will be looking to hire law students that have a demonstrated interest in the field of law they practice, in addition to good grades and a winning personality. The variable time frame above exacerbates this issue, as if you apply for a job in a particular niche, you may get an employment offer relatively quickly, and you will have to make the decision whether or not to accept. To be sure, though, while you are still looking, you can and should advocate that your background is relevant to multiple specialties.

ii. Strategies for Getting a Job Outside of OCI

1. Keep It Personal

While this is a digital age, personal connections are best when you need people to help you, and in engaging in the arduous task of seeking a job as an attorney outside of OCI, you should unabashedly seek others' help. In engaging in your search, you should aim to connect positively with as many people that might in any way be able to help you in your search and suppress any feelings you have that reaching out is awkward or will not help. For example:

- You should scour your friends and family to identify every person you know or they know that is a lawyer or can introduce you to lawyers.

- You should reach out to current and former law students, alumni of your college, and even of your high school or people from your hometown who are lawyers or may know lawyers. While stereotypically having a connection to a rainmaking partner is the best way to work a connection, the reality is that clients are much more important to firms than almost any partner, and a recommendation from a businessperson to their outside counsel can go a long way.

- You should talk to anyone you know that works for an employer of attorneys, such as a government agency, even if they are not an attorney, as they may know of openings or be able to identify them.

- You should engage with your local bar associations as a student member, try to join a committee, and in general present yourself as a smart and poised young individual who would make a great hire.

- You should frequently go on informational interviews to speak to successful practicing attorneys, tell them about yourself, and seek their guidance.

- Law professors are an obvious audience for assistance as well if you have a good relationship with them.

- Engage in internships to increase your visibility and experience level.

Some of this may sound like begging, but you should work these relationships with confidence. The most important thing to realize when engaging in this process is that most people want to help other people when they can. They may not have an opportunity at their firm, or they may not even want to recommend you for it, but they hopefully may know someone else that may have a better opportunity. You may even get people to push your case to their peers. For example, some lawyers network on email listservs with others in the same niche; someone may be willing to mention your name anonymously in case others are looking for an entry-level attorney.

Moreover, this outreach really involves little other than shooting the breeze. No one will expect you as a law student to be an expert or have any meaningful legal experience; the most you can do is be likable and professional. To be sure, the more you become generally familiar with the various niches that the lawyers you reach out to are practicing, the more they will be impressed and view you as a relatively sophisticated student, but little more than what is printed in this book is necessary for that purpose. After the interaction, be it at a cocktail reception or at an informational interview, take a business card, connect to them on LinkedIn (no Facebook...you have to be kidding), and be sure to follow up in the future as appropriate.

2. Don't Forget About the Impersonal

Of course, many positions are available on the web, and you should exploit all available digital resources in your search as well. This obviously includes your law school website, and you should be sure to ask your friends in other schools if they are aware of positions posted at their school. Outside of those curated websites, this book will not attempt to categorize the burgeoning mess of legal and generalized job search websites except to state the obvious that you should review them for openings, while identifying connections at the organization in question to actually submit your application. There are also websites that usefully aggregate openings posted on different legal websites, although there may be subscription fees.

3. Other Strategies - Go Where They 'Aint

Outside of executing the compound extrovert-personal connection / introvert-Web search outlined above, you should also try where possible to seek jobs in ways that others are not. While this is a generalized point, I specify this advice in two ways. First, consider rural or otherwise not highly competitive geographic areas. Many sources have noted that such areas are not only not swamped with lawyers but suffer from a dearth of them.[22] Of

---

[22] http://www.washingtonpost.com/news/storyline/wp/2014/08/25/how-do-you-keep-them-down-on-the-farm-once-theyve-passed-the-bar/?utm_term=.600f2a83f7eb.

course, geographic areas that qualify as rural may not be your first (or second or third) choice, but you may find that the combination of a good job and an excellent lifestyle makes taking such a position one of the best choices you ever make.

Second, be sure to continue your job search after you obtain a position, especially for jobs at small firms that may be relatively unstable or other types of employment that you would rather not have. You should continue to network heavily and keep your eyes and ears open - discreetly of course - as you begin your new job. Those that do may find another position that is much more to their liking come their way, while those that don't may be rudely dismissed from a small firm and forced to begin a job search from scratch while unemployed, or find themselves becoming overly seasoned in an industry or type of employer at which they do not want to remain. Ultimately, only you will own your own career, and you owe it to yourself to own it 24-7-365.

Chapter 8: Second/Third Year

After completing the legendary first year of law school, you should be beaming with pride at what you have accomplished. Essentially, you have just ridden to the top of the law school hill and, while you still have to pedal back downhill, the rest of the way will not be nearly as aching. Soon, you may even not have to listen to my random metaphors!

While the last two years are not nearly as nerve-wracking and unique as the first year, you should still carefully think about a plan for how to approach these years, which ultimately include 2/3 of your law school GPA. In this chapter, I first analyze popular conceptions, true and imaginary, on the differences between the first year and the last two. I then discuss various issues arising out of the second and third year of law school, including how to approach which courses to take, whether and to what extent to get involved in extra-curricular activities, how to get involved in non-academic pursuits such as internships, and, while as mentioned previously this book is not a study guide, approaching the Bar.

a. Differences Between First Year and Last Two Years

The second and third year of law school is in some ways a whiplash reversal from the ultra-intensity of the fixed requirements of the first year. You will still have the same amount of classes, but as opposed to the traditional common law courses that the school requires you to take during your first year, during your second and third year you will have a broad range of options, largely up to your discretion. Courses available to you include those focused on industry and practice-area specific issues as well as on more theoretical areas of legal thought. Far from the Socratic pressure-cooker atmosphere that some first-year courses can create, many of your second and third-year courses will be conducted in a relatively relaxed seminar atmosphere, and may not even include a final exam. While first-year courses can seem extraordinarily theoretical, during your second and third years you will likely have the option to receive credit for working at a law school legal clinic where you can practically apply your legal knowledge and skills towards a range of legal representations.

However, the oft-claimed distinction that during your last two years in law school you don't need to work hard and ensure good grades in your courses is only true in a limited sense and in certain cases. Certainly, for those students, which probably constitute the majority if not a strong majority of law students in the country, who did not receive an offer to join a large law firm's summer program during their third semester of law school, doing well remains paramount. Such students will need another internship during their second summer and may be interviewing for entry-level positions during their third year or after graduation. While first-year grades will be the only way to achieve some academic honors such as Law Review, employers reviewing transcripts at such a time will not limit their review to first-year grades. Indeed, in such a situation, employers may actually look more favorably at students who continually improved their grades over their law school career than those who started strong but slipped during the second and/or third year.

Even for those students fortunate to have received an offer to join a summer associate program at a large law firm, there are many reasons to keep up the hard work. Yes, the probability is that, assuming no major blowups on their part, these students will receive an offer to rejoin the firm following graduation. Yes, barring truly poor grades, most law firm will extend offers to otherwise acceptable summer associates regardless of grades received during the second year.

However, there are several other reasons for continuing to excel. First, students that continue to do well with be eligible for numerous academic honors, including cum laude honors and graduation awards. Doing well is also important, in some cases essential, to a variety of employment opportunities, both entry-level and for experienced lawyers, other than working as a first year associate at a large law firm. In addition, the honors noted above look very good on a resume, and will, in particular, be helpful if one looks to exit out of one's initial job. When you look to make such a move, even if you attended an elite school, the initial need on many firms' part to hire a lot of entry-level associates from elite schools will dissipate, and you will need to further explain why you are unique even from the many others looking for a much smaller set of positions available to experienced attorneys, even those from such schools. Honors can help with that narrative.

Academic excellence will be particularly important for those students interested in public service. One will only be able to interview for clerkships in the third year, and many students clerk only after working in a law firm for a couple of years. As a result, grades are important if you are interested in those positions either immediately or in the future. In addition, most entry-level government jobs will also only be available to third year students, and many government employers, certainly including prestigious employers such as U.S. Attorneys' offices, will request a transcript even for applicants that are experienced lawyers. These employers expect to see a continuous record of academic success, especially in courses most relevant to their work.

Ultimately, unless you are attempting to work part-time every available second, you should have the time necessary, on an efficient basis, to study sufficiently to do well in your second and third-year courses. You owe it to yourself to use that time wisely and study.

b. Coursework

As mentioned above, one of the features of the last two years of law school you will enjoy is almost unlimited freedom in choosing your course load. How should you exercise your discretion?

Many law students look to continue taking foundational courses in legal doctrine. I would generally recommend a couple of courses in this vein, but keep it limited to your particular areas of interest. For example, if you are intent on a litigation career and have future aspirations of serving as a prosecutor, evidence, and criminal procedure courses are a must, but corporations and securities regulation can be passed up, and vice versa for a future corporate dealmaker.

Similarly, the view that you should take at least a couple of basic courses in your area of interest is well taken, but there's no need to focus exclusively on such courses. The problem with taking too many of these courses is that many to most of them are unforgivingly graded on the same type of curve as your first-year courses. While hopefully you will ace every one of these you take, the competition will remain fierce, even at elite schools, and the more you take the more likely you will receive lower grades. Employers, on the whole, will base their view of your academic success exclusively on GPA and will simply not excuse a lower GPA based on the argument that harder coursework was taken.

As a result, it is a good idea to choose several courses that are not graded on a curve and/or you otherwise have a good chance of receiving a good grade. First-year courses are usually graded on an unforgiving curve - there's nothing you can do about that. Now that your first-year grades are in, however, the ball is more in your court to shape what grades you receive. Seminar-style courses are more likely to be graded on a basis other than a curve, and certain professors will likely also be more relaxed about grades than others. Avoiding yet another Socratic course graded on a curve to keep up your GPA even though it is relevant for your legal career, or interesting, is certainly rational, as getting good grades is much more important for your career than any individual course.

One additional question is whether to take courses you are interested in, regardless of practical importance or ease. You can certainly do so, but you should take into consideration practical importance and grades as well. Ultimately, law school is not a theoretical, purist intellectual exercise - it's a degree for which you are paying tens of thousands of dollars. You can learn about art law all you want on your own time without having to pull a C from a nasty 90-year-old professor who didn't like what you had to say about a certain case.

c. Extracurricular Activities

A related question to how hard to work in courses is whether it is worth it to engage in the many extra-curricular activities available to law students, such as student committees, legal clinics, moot court, and the like. Many schools only give students the option of taking on these activities in the last two years, and certainly all students have more time to do so during those years.

Regarding these activities, ultimately you should take on as much, or as little, as you have interest and bandwidth, without impacting your grades or your job search. In terms of practical importance, while these activities can, like many things, help enhance your resume, their absence will not hurt your resume in a profound way. These extracurricular activities could potentially provide you with helpful legal skills and networking opportunities, and if you win a moot court competition or similar, that is a great honor to list, but in most cases there are alternative ways to provide anything helpful from these activities. Serving as an officer of the Law and Business student group may help you develop an interest in corporate law, but significant coursework in that area of law or working part-time in the field as an intern will do the same if not much more effectively, in addition to providing you a significant amount of knowledge.

Ultimately, many students enjoy these activities and if you have the time, by all means, pursue them. But if you have competing interests, don't worry that you are hurting your resume or chances of future employment in any material way.

The one exception are activities where you can develop a relationship with professors and industry professionals. There are several such opportunities potentially available to law school students. Professors offer teacher assistant positions to some high-achieving students for them to provide review sessions to first-year students. Such positions are prestigious and reflect well on you for multiple reasons. It shows that not only have you succeeded academically, but you also have been able to forge a professional relationship with the professor and have the ability to work with both the professor, your boss, and subordinates (i.e. your students) in a leadership role. This is excellent training and an excellent credential for a future role in a variety of legal fields. Other opportunities to work with a professor involve less public roles, such as serving as a research assistant during the year. If you have the bandwidth and interest, and are considering clerkships or government positions, you should not pass up opportunities such as these to develop a strong relationship with a future recommender.

One additional opportunity that I encourage you to consider will require you to reach out to the professor rather than the opposite - working on a law review article together. Many law schools require students to draft a long written piece of legal scholarship. Once you have invested the significant time and effort to draft this piece, there is no reason not to also submit it to law reviews and other legal journals for potential publication. Getting published in a law review is a meaningful accomplishment and reflects well on you, as it indicates that you have excellent written communication skills and have the ability to put in the sufficient diligence, thoughtfulness, and follow-through necessary to produce a published piece of legal scholarship.

Publishing is also not all that hard to do. First, you should certainly try to get published in your own schools' journals. However, even if that fails, there are many of these publications - every law school has at least one student-edited legal publication and most have several - which means that, depending on what school you attend, how hard you worked on your article, and how many journals you submit to, your chances of getting published are much higher than what you might think. Submitting also does not take up a significant amount of time, given that these journals have set up online submission systems that allow you to submit to numerous journals in an efficient manner, and submitting is also relatively inexpensive or free if you are a law student.

While getting published in and of itself is not extremely difficult, where "the game" resides is in getting published in a journal that is higher in the "pecking order." The first distinction is between flagship law reviews and other legal periodicals. For each law school that sponsors more than one journal, there will typically be one flagship journal, typically but not always known as a "law review," along with other journals. These other journals frequently but always are limited in subject matter to a particular area of law. Getting published in a school's law review is much harder, and more prestigious, than getting published in a school's other legal journals. Another distinction is based on which school is sponsoring the legal journal. Professors regard some law reviews with more interest than others. While there is an online ranking specifically focused on law reviews,[23] all else being equal, you can generally assume that the higher the U.S. News ranking for a particular law school, the more highly regarded its legal journals are.

Thus, it is considered a bigger accomplishment to be published in a flagship law review and in a higher-ranked school, and this is where professors can be helpful. Regardless of how rigorously researched and expertly written your article is, many law reviews are much more interested in publishing articles written by actual recognized professors than law students. If a professor lends his or her name as a co-author to your article, your chances of publication, and especially publication in a more prestigious journal, are greatly increased.

d. Work

In addition to coursework and extracurricular activities, the last two years are also different in their allowance for students to spend a relatively meaningful amount of time working for pay. A wide variety of employers seek law student legal help during the school year, including law firms, financial firms, and corporations. This is a robust opportunity for several reasons.

To start, the pay provided by these employers varies wildly but can be quite generous. At the top of the market, if you served as a summer associate at a large law firm and they need extra help, they may provide you the

---

[23] http://lawlib.wlu.edu/LJ/

opportunity to work on an hourly basis during the school year as well. You will need to privately inquire about these opportunities during your summer, but the pay is very generous and in line, on a pro-rata basis, with compensation received by first-year associates. Outside of such opportunities, which are relatively rare, many mid-size and boutique law firms advertise for law student help. Compensation, responsibility, and work environment varies just as wildly for such firms as it does for summer internships, and you could earn anywhere from $15 to $100 per hour.

If you could use the money, I recommend looking for such opportunities, as long as you keep a healthy work-school balance in check. Working is the potential counterweight to the concern mentioned earlier about racking up debt for living expenses during law school, and earning part-time income gives you the opportunity to limit your loan burden. You may also get practical training in tasks such as research and writing in which you will be expected to excel as a junior associate.

In addition, while it is certainly the path with the most options, by no means should you limit your consideration of part-time employment to legal work. There may be several other avenues, depending on your schedule, your prior work experience, and your skills, for remunerative work. If you excelled on the LSAT, consider serving as an LSAT tutor or teacher. Perhaps, your employer, prior to law school, could use extra help, or you may even have opportunities to wait tables at exclusive restaurants. While none of these options may be prestigious, I can assure you that you will not care about that when you start to pay down your loans and realize how much more you would have had to pay per month if you hadn't worked.

To be sure, you should balance your workload with your course load, but the level of equilibrium you reach is ultimately dependent on your circumstances. For those students without an offer from a large law firm, ensuring that you have the time and energy to excel in your studies is absolutely essential, as by far the most important criteria to future employers is GPA, and the impact of poor grades during your second or third year will not be lessened by work experience, however relevant.

However, for those students who have received an offer from a large law firm, and you are intent on returning to that firm and do not have an interest in future positions such as clerkships or government work where grades again become relevant, I would be comfortable devoting more time to remunerative work even if you may not receive straight A's. To be sure, you should still make sure to keep up your grades, but in this case you are balancing cold hard loan reduction with a very ephemeral and vague benefit of excellent grades, perhaps reflected in graduation honors.

e. The Bar

This is it. The end of the road. The final challenge. (That is, before the really hard stuff like work starts.)

The Bar is at once both an imposing challenge - a comprehensive test of legal memorization and analysis demanding months of study from even the most highly intelligent students - and an overhyped stepping stone that, given the extremely high passage rates in many states, you should be less concerned about than you might think. The statistics make this clear - in New York state, a whopping 83% of students from ABA-approved law schools passed the Bar exam on average from 2004-2016.[24] I am told that, when you eliminate students for whom English is a second language, that figure rises to 90%.

Those numbers are quite unlike the fierce zero-sum game you are used to from the LSAT and law school. On the Bar, the old medical school yarn (Q. What do you call the person who scores the lowest passing score on the Medical Boards? A: A doctor) also rings true. From the perspective of there being zero benefits to doing relatively well on the test, the Bar may be the least important test that you have taken since you started college.

---

[24] https://www.nybarexam.org/ExamStats/NYBarExam_AnnualPassRates%20_2004-2016.pdf.

On the other hand, a blasé attitude is probably not the best approach. Passage rates in some states, such as Florida[25] and California[26], are much lower. Further, even if 99% passed, at the end of the day you decidedly do not want to be the 1% that does not, regardless of how well you have done to date. For those who do not have a job as they study for the Bar, this goes without saying, but it is equally true for those that do. You may lose your job for failing the Bar, and you certainly will if you fail twice.

Ultimately, you do need to approach the Bar very seriously; you just don't need to be anxious or nervous. You, like the vast majority of your fellow ~~students~~ graduates (!), can do this.

Oh, okay, good ... But, wait, how???? Although I mentioned above that this is not an exam study guide, I am happy to provide my A-Z list of Bar exam tips (each of which you must follow or you will fail).

Study Plan/Preparation

a. *Take Bar-Bri.*
There are several very good reasons why it has been the top Bar review course for many years. It hires highly engaging teachers, several of whom were among the best teachers I have ever had, that make attending lectures truly enjoyable. It has comprehensive materials. Most importantly, it has created a moat through the very amount of students attending it, which gives the company unparalleled insight into and feedback from the bar exam. It costs a lot, but failing costs a lot more.

b. *Don't be radical in the material you use.*
Remember that you just need to finish in the top 90%. That crackpot friend of yours who has some wildly unorthodox set of outlines and study methods? Using those materials could mean you finish in the top 5% - but what will that do for you? It could also mean you are missing

---

[25]https://www.floridabarexam.org/__85257bfe0055eb2c.nsf/52286ae9ad5d84518525 7c07005c3fe1/95960882122575be85258034004be367
[26]http://admissions.calbar.ca.gov/Portals/4/documents/Statistics/JULY2016STATS1 20716_R.pdf.

the material that most other students are studying and will finish poorly, perhaps dangerously so. This is another support for taking Bar-Bri - given how many other students use Bar-Bri, you will be studying the material that the most other students are studying. If you master the material they give, even if that material is, in certain situations, less "test-like," you will be right in the middle of a large crowd of similarly situated others who will know and not know exactly what you know and don't know. In such a situation, you likely pass the test by a comfortable margin.

c. *On the other hand, customize the suggested study schedule and materials to your needs.*
Go to live classes or Web video based on how well you pay attention; while being sure to keep up, study in the hours that work for you, and most importantly focus on the areas of law that you need to work on the most.

d. *You don't need to study all the time, but start early and keep your study schedule consistent.*
Treat studying for the bar like a job (a normal job, not a crazy legal job). Clock in at a normal time in the morning and feel free to clock out at a normal time in the early evening. Just don't spend weeks avoiding the exam or finding excuses to avoid studying along the way. That will make the inevitable freak-out (see below) much stronger.

e. *Please don't "pre-clerk."*
Pre-clerking is working at a large law firm as a summer associate during part of the same summer you study for the Bar. Working as a summer associate is a time-intensive and, more importantly, emotionally demanding experience all by itself; combining it with bar study, while possible, is crazy talk. While you can and should be doing something other than studying all day and night, I would recommend something less all-consuming than a summer program. At the very least, make sure

to devote 100% of your time during the last month before the test to the test.

Study Mechanics

f. *Full-length practice tests aren't helpful.*
You are quite used to long tests by now and don't need endurance training. Understand the format of the test and focus on building your knowledge and skills.

g. *However, practicing how to write answers to essay questions is very helpful.*
Like with law school exams, you will not be able to truly assess your knowledge and your abilities in applying it to the essay questions until you actually write out the essays. It's much easier just to study, but writing is essential. Write many essays, or risk never realizing what you need to work on both in terms of format and knowledge-building.

h. *Memorize.*
With regard to forcing yourself to do the hard tasks, make sure to actually memorize the material rather than just reading or writing it. Say it over in your mind until you know it without looking - backward in Swedish.

i. *Don't freak out if Bar-Bri flunks your essay.*
If you submit essays for grading to a test prep operator, please know that they grade harder than the Bar exam graders do.

j. *Do freak out if you're not passing the MBE practice tests.*
On the other hand, your MBE practice score needs to be meaningfully higher than passing in order for you to feel confident in being able to pass. You have to assume doing slightly worse in the heat of test day.

k. *Divide and conquer.*
   For most of the time spent studying, focus on your areas of weakness. However, near the end, focus on your strengths, as if you haven't gotten it until now you probably won't get it now. Further, focusing on strengths near the end will also help reduce and not increase your anxiety right before test day.

l. *Avoid groups and study buddies.*
   This advice applies whether or not you found study groups helpful in law school. Law school is unique because every test and every professor is different, and study groups can help you navigate the different approaches. The Bar, on the other hand, is standardized.

m. *Focus on the material that your study guides present as being necessary for the test.*
   There may be various gaps that you identify and you may worry that you are not fully understanding the subject. Relax. Just know what you have to know.

n. *Try to see joy and humor in the material as much as possible.*
   This will help your sanity, your focus, and your memory. There's a reason many speakers start with a joke. This is another reason to take Bar-Bri, whose professors are frequently hilarious.

o. *Make the material your own.*
   Mark up your study guides and verbalize the material, even to yourself. This helps reinforce memory.

Sanity and Focus

p. *Keep in contact with non-lawyer friends and family.*
   You, and others in your shoes, will be entering a weird reality for the next couple of months. It's always helpful for your sanity to retain relationships to some of the still-sane seven billion other people in the world.

q. Please be advised that, no matter how hard you study *you will have a serious freak-out at some point.*

For me, it was July 4th weekend - less than a month before the test, when I received poor grades on my essays and my MBE scores were not nearly where I wanted them to be. For a couple of days, I was a wreck. Expect it to happen, so that when it happens it won't be that bad. But it will be bad.

r. Oh, by the way, *the entire last month before the test will be hell,* perhaps one of the worst months in your life.

The importance of passing the test, the sheer amount of information, the mind-numbing obscurity of the information needed to be mastered, and the need to master all of it while still remaining alive and sentient will be exhausting and maddening. Look to the test as your release date from the insane asylum, and its approach will be more like a joyous occasion and not impending doom.

s. *Stay healthy.*

To keep yourself relatively balanced, be absolutely sure to eat healthy food and exercise regularly (a few times per week) throughout your bar study period. This will, in turn, help you sleep regularly as well.

t. *A low level of tension and nervousness is to be expected.*

However, if you are feeling constantly anxious and it is interfering with or preventing you at times from studying, you need to nip this in the bud as soon as possible. Exercise every day, have fun with your friends, and get your mind off of the test for a meaningful amount of time per week. If that doesn't work, seek professional counseling to fix this so you can have at least the end of your summer focused on studying, but in a productive manner.

u. Remember that all of this is not dry, it is not theoretical, and it is not meaningless - it is *your ticket to an exciting, lucrative, and prestigious career.*

Test Day

v. *Take the day off before the exam.*
Exercise, go out with your (non-lawyer) friends or family, and think about anything other than law, lawyers, or the bar exam, and especially do not think about the rule against perpetuities, whatever you do.

w. *Read the technical aspects of your test site and make sure you have your laptop or another technical setup one week before the exam.* Prepare everything else (food, pencils) at least two days before so you can have the last day to zone out per above.

x. *Only talk to nice, non-competitive people during the exam.*
If you don't know any students like that, or you're not sure, just don't talk to anyone. The anxiety created by jerks who like to make other people insecure is real and potentially impactful on a test like this, depending on your personality.

y. *Do not think for a second about the Bar exam after you take it.*
You are done and there's nothing else to do. Wait until you see your score, and worry about what you did wrong only if and when you learn that you have failed.

z. *That's it, there aren't any other tips. You're really done. With everything.*
As you finish up studying for the Bar, and certainly after you take it, it will dawn on you that you have just completed not just an examination but an entire part of your life - the part devoted to education. To have received a law degree, you will have had to complete at least 19 years of education. That's a long time. And after the Bar, most law graduates will never formally enroll as a student in an educational institution every again. You are now entering a completely new chapter - the one devoted to employment. For those of you who disliked school, this may be a relief, but you are sure at some point to look wistfully at your many

years of relatively straight-forward student life, not having to worry about bosses, coworkers, retaining a job or getting a better one. You may miss the intellectual challenge that school provided. However, let's be real - you will certainly not miss the Ramen. On to the big bucks - entering the legal profession!

PART 3

Successfully Entering the Legal Profession

Chapter 9: Types of Practice Areas

The legal field has increasingly become an amalgam of various sub-specialty niches rather than one unified profession, as clients and employers have increasingly looked to specifically relevant experience in deciding who to hire. It is increasingly difficult to switch from one niche to another and, therefore, it is very important to understand the various niches as you make your initial search for employment.

There is a brief summary of each of the most important niches below, as well as an analysis of the extent the jobs in such fields are available to law students unable to secure a summer associate position.[27] This analysis, however, will also help educate students who are going to be serving as summer associates to understand the various fields in which law firms practice.

The below lists and analyzes each of the various legal fields and ranks these fields in various ways. First, it denotes (with a checkmark) those that are open to a wider variety of graduates. Second, it ranks each of the fields on a 1-4 scale based on how lucrative they are to law firms, with a 1 being the most lucrative and 4 being those fields in which large law firms generally do not practice. More lucrative fields will be hotly pursued by even the most prestigious law firms, while such firms will leave less lucrative fields to less prestigious firms. Finally, it notes (with an "N" for "niche") those niches that provide relatively little work and, thus, there will be relatively few jobs available regardless of pedigree.

Antitrust 2

Antitrust transactional lawyers provide counseling to companies and investors on how to structure their corporate development and investment activities, with a particular focus on mergers & acquisitions, to avoid

---

[27] There are, of course, numerous smaller niches that this book does not analyze due to lack of space and relative lack of relevance to many law students.

scrutiny by trade regulators, such as the Federal Trade Commission in the US as well as regulators in other jurisdictions such as the European Union. Such lawyers also advocate for and even litigate on behalf of their clients if these regulators seek to stop activities or mergers. Antitrust practice, while complex, is sometimes seen as a way to support a mergers & acquisitions practice rather than a true money-maker; while the area is relatively small, it provides a meaningful amount of jobs and has meaningful exit opportunities, including work in government. However, your options will be concentrated in firms located in the big population centers, especially NYC and DC.

There are also a few lawyers that focus on antitrust litigation, in which private companies sue other companies accusing them of unfair trade practices. While such litigation is high-stakes and complex, there are relatively few lawyers practicing in this niche.

Appellate 2, N

These lawyers specialize in litigating cases at a court of appeal or even the Supreme Court. Don't let the "2" fool you - this practice area is perhaps the most highly competitive legal field of any kind. You will need to have an appellate clerkship even to be considered for specialization in this area. The competition will be brutal even after you begin your career, not to mention that high-stakes nature of the actual work. Apply only if you are both a brainiac and not faint of heart.

While there are some jobs in this field in many parts of the country, jobs specialized exclusively in appellate litigation tend to congregate in DC and a couple other geographic areas where highly important cases are litigated. Many elite New York law firms, on the other hand, represent clients on appellate matters as part of a general litigation practice but avoid specializing in this area (hence the "2"), as appellate work does not require a lot of associates, given that once the case is at the appellate level the record of documents and testimony is final and only the proper procedure and law is at issue.

Bankruptcy 2

As a bankruptcy lawyer, you will represent creditors or debtors in negotiating to resolve situations that could lead to bankruptcy, or in actual bankruptcy litigation proceedings. Bankruptcy practice requires a broad range of skills and is a unique blend of transactional and litigation practice. As part of your work, you will be interfacing regularly with your colleagues in the mergers & acquisition, lending, and litigation practice groups. Like tax law, bankruptcy practice centers around a particular body of law, the federal bankruptcy code, but bankruptcy law is less abstract and doctrinal than tax law and succeeding in bankruptcy work requires a greater dose of shrewd negotiating and advocacy skills than subject matter expertise. Bankruptcy practice groups retain their own clients in addition to supporting other practice groups. It is highly profitable work generally, in part because service providers such as law firms get paid first out of a bankruptcy, but it is also very cyclical.

Blue Collar Criminal Defense 4 √

Representing criminal defendants in matters other than corporate or white collar offenses is a relatively non-lucrative practice that large law firms do not engage in. Clients may have little resources, making even collecting bills a challenge at times. However, the work will certainly be highly engaging and may involve a lot of courtroom experience.

Class Action Defense 2

Attorneys in these practice areas defend corporations and financial institutions, generally public companies, against litigations where plaintiffs' attorneys (see Class actions - Plaintiff) seek to represent a class of people allegedly harmed by the company pursuant to Rule 23 of the Federal Rules of Civil Procedure or equivalent state rules. Class action litigations most frequently allege damages accruing from defective products, mass torts, or violations of the securities laws, state corporate law, or employment law. If a court allows the plaintiff (and his or her attorney) to represent the class - what is called "certifying" the class - the potential damages against the company are exponentially more than the amount any litigation with individually named plaintiffs could deliver, which makes the practice area potentially very lucrative to the attorney seeking to represent the class given that he or she can now collect attorney's fees on the larger amount.

On the defense side, while this practice area has become somewhat less lucrative due to limitations the Supreme Court has placed on the types of class actions that can be brought, it remains a cash cow due to the number of attorneys filing litigations in which they seek to represent classes. Generally, only large law firms will be involved in this practice area due to the frequently large amount of documents and fact issues such cases involve.

Class Actions - Plaintiff 4 √

Attorneys representing the plaintiff side of the "v" in class actions seek to identify a potential class of people or investors for which a credible claim can be made that they were wronged by a large corporation or financial institution, identify a client to serve as the lead plaintiff to represent the class, and then prosecute the claim against the defendant and get the class certified. As you might surmise, this "practice area" has enriched lawyers more than class members in many cases, and both Congress and the court system has taken steps to limit the types of class actions that can be successfully brought and what access such actions will have to documents and testimony in early stages of the litigation. That being said, a successful plaintiffs side attorney can make multiple times what he or she would make as a partner at a large law firm. While the work can be demanding at times, it does not involve the types of time pressures that (real) clients provide.

Corporate Compliance / Governance 1

This practice advises the public and other companies and financial institutions on proper corporate governance, compliance with state corporate law and the federal securities laws, and various other regulatory schemes applicable to such firms. Clients highly prize this advice and thus willingly pay high billing rates for it. However, as it does not require a large amount of associate support, attorneys giving such advice tend to perform other legal work, such as general corporate transactional work like M&A, in addition.

Elder / Medicaid / Social Security Disability 4 √

In this niche, you advise older individuals on navigating the various regulatory and wealth planning issues that arise as they get older, including deciding how to pass on or give away their wealth and other resources, access long-term care, and navigate Medicare, Social Security (disability and generally), and Medicaid. You will deal with some of the same issues as those who work in a trusts & estates practice, but those practices are generally more complex as they represent high net worth individuals and thus will touch issues that practices working with less rich people will not present.

Employee Benefits / ERISA 2

This practice area relates to the Employment Retirement Investment Security Act, known by the acronym ERISA, and the rules and regulations and case law regarding ERISA. ERISA lawyers frequently consult on mergers and other transactions and advise companies and investment funds on complying with ERISA law. Given the high stakes that violating ERISA presents, large law firms generally have ERISA practices but these practices generally support other practices within the firm rather than retaining independent clients. Similar to bankruptcy law, ERISA is a subject-matter expertise that is less complex than tax law, but unlike bankruptcy law, it involves only advisory rather than litigation practice; while there is litigation that involves ERISA, general litigators usually handle that litigation, perhaps with support from ERISA lawyers.

Environmental 3, N

Attorneys in this practice area advise on compliance with federal, state, and local environmental law and regulations. There are very few lawyers in this practice area at even the largest law firms; although many boutiques also practice this area of law and the billing rates are relatively high, there is less work available than other specialties.

Family 4 √

As a family lawyer, you will represent parties in a divorce, child custody, and other family status proceedings and litigation and negotiate settlements to these issues. While there are, of course, numerous cases regarding family law, it tends to be more about fierce courtroom battles and wily negotiating tactics rather than cerebral research, given that it is so fact-specific and tends to be litigated in courts with less erudite judges.

Financial Services Regulation 1

Companies and firms that provide investment or financial services are subject to a dizzying array of laws, rules, and regulations promulgated by an alphabet soup of federal and state regulators. The stakes are very high, and clients tend to be highly profitable and willing to provide very high billing rates for advice related to these regulations. Jobs in this area may require wonkish familiarity with these regulations but will provide excellent exit options, including in-house and government jobs. However, it is easiest to specialize in this area for those attorneys in geographic financial centers and the most prestigious firms that boast large financial institutions as clients, while practitioners in other geographic areas and at other firms will more likely combine this practice with other work such as structuring transactions.

First Amendment 2 N

First Amendment work involves litigating cases involving questions regarding freedom of speech and religious freedom. This work can be extraordinarily high-profile and interesting, but the number of firms that boast a focus area in this area is vanishingly small.

General Commercial Transactions 3 C

In addition to specific types of episodic transactions such as mergers and loans, companies - big and small - hire lawyers to advise on general commercial agreements and transactions. Such work is steady but decreasing in value due to increasing realization on the parts of clients as to how little they can get by paying for such services, given how many lawyers perform these services and increasing in-sourcing of the work to in-house attorneys and alternative legal services providers.

Government Contracts and Lobbying 2 N

Some law firms, almost exclusively in DC, lobby on behalf of their clients to the federal government and advise on contracts with the government. This is lucrative work, but generally, the most prestigious firms do not engage in it. It is also generally not available in other areas of the country.

Government Enforcement / White Collar Criminal 1

This area of the law represents individuals, businesses, and financial institutions in civil and criminal investigations of violations of law, generally by federal regulators and prosecutors in addition to state attorneys' general. As blue-collar criminal prosecutions began to decline in the late 1990s, prosecutor offices began focusing more heavily on white-collar crime and found numerous violations, a growth trend that has continued unabated to the present.

This practice area is one of the most lucrative for large law firms both because of the huge demand and also because the investigations frequently require large teams to produce and analyze a large quantity of documents, comb the facts and present arguments to the government. Clients are willing to pay hefty fees due to the enormous damage such investigations can do to their bottom line both directly and indirectly via reputational damage. Numerous boutiques also work in this space. Lateral opportunities to prosecutors or regulatory offices abound; there are also a growing number of in-house opportunities seeking specialists in the area, but such opportunities are generally highly competitive. One limitation on career growth for associates in this practice area is that many firms only name partners in this specialty who have previously worked for the government.

Government Regulatory (non-financial services) 2 N

There are various federal, state, and local regulatory schemes that companies seek to comply with and occasionally seek to change. For example, some firms advise clients on specialized transactions in the healthcare industry and on the numerous regulations that companies in the health field face. Another niche practice advises companies in the natural resource industry (i.e. utilities/water/timber/mining) on various regulatory issues relating to such industries as well as engaging with the government on their behalf; this practice area is generally limited to firms in the geographic areas where such companies are located.

It is hard to generalize about such a broad array of practices, but each of the practices individually are relatively small.

Immigration 4 √

In immigration law, you represent individuals in immigration applications and proceedings and counseling companies with regard to business-related immigration laws. This area of law is generally practiced by solo practitioners or small law firms, and the path to making a meaningful amount of money is generally by making partner or starting your own firm, as associate positions generally don't pay that much and there are no in-house options available. Like with elder law, part of the trouble in being successful in immigration law is that most of the work involves counseling individual people and many of the people seeking these services are not wealthy, and thus unable to afford high billing rates. Indeed, many law firms provide the neediest individuals with pro bono immigration assistance, particularly with regard to applications for asylum visas.

Intellectual Property 1 (litigation and transactional), 3 √ (registration)

Intellectual property (IP) law concerns the body of federal law regulating patents, copyrights, and trademarks. While there are several sub-specialties within IP law, it is, in general, a steady practice area that rewards practitioners richly for performing work that is highly technical and complex.

While every industry uses intellectual property protections, certain industries, including life sciences and technology, use IP attorneys more heavily. IP is the primary asset for businesses in these industries and IP assets can be worth millions or billions of dollars in many cases to companies in these industries. Law firms and in-house employers will prefer attorneys with bachelors, masters or even Ph.Ds. in the sciences or technology over those who do not, and in many cases such degrees are required.

Attorneys practice IP work in three contexts - seeking registration of IP from the federal government, litigation, and IP advisory with regard to transactions such as mergers & acquisitions. Registration work is relatively commoditized and attracts lower billing rates than many other areas of law. IP litigation can be worth millions or billions of dollars and involve extraordinarily complex facts and as a result, many large law firms have grown their IP litigation practices considerably. The practice of many law firms in advising on IP aspects of transactions has also grown considerably and attracts high billing rates.

Investment Management 1

Attorneys in this field advise public (i.e. mutual funds) and private (i.e. private equity and hedge funds) investment funds and investment advisers on creating and managing their funds and businesses, engaging in transactions, and complying with federal securities regulation. This is a massively profitable niche for numerous law firms as such funds frequently open (and close), there is significant capital provided by investors to such funds, fund clients are willing to pay top dollar in terms of billing rates, and there are significant cross-selling opportunities between this practice and other practices of the firm, such as M&A and lending, that can also service investment management clients. Some firms provide different attorneys for the regulatory advisory work involved in the practice and for structuring funds and fund transactions, while others combine these two areas into a single practice group.

Labor and Employment 3 C

This practice area involves all three types of legal practice - advisory, transactional, and litigation. On the advisory side, labor lawyers counsel businesses with regard to compliance with federal, state, and local labor laws - for instance, in crafting compliant employee manuals. On the transaction side, individuals and businesses seek guidance in executing employment, separation, collective bargaining and other agreements and transactions with unions, executives, and other employees. On the litigation side, labor lawyers represent both plaintiffs and defendants in employment-related lawsuits, including claims for violations of the federal discrimination laws. The litigation side of the practice blossomed when courts began allowing punitive damages for employment claims, but in the last couple of decades, large law firms have moved away from this practice towards more document-heavy financial litigation that commands higher billing rates and requires more associate support; the billing rates today are much lower than for many other areas of law.

Generally, solo practitioners and small law firms will represent plaintiffs and unions while mid-size and larger law firms will represent businesses, although even the largest law firms will also represent employees that are senior executives. In some law firms, the same lawyers practice both labor/employment law, primarily in an advisory capacity, as well as ERISA practice.

Lending/Finance 1

Almost every company carries some debt, and debt financing is a crucial piece of the capital structure of many of the most complex transactions. Financing transactions can be quite complex and take numerous forms, and thus require careful legal advice and documentation. Lending transactions are certainly considered one of the most important practice areas to many clients and, in turn, to many firms, including the biggest and most prestigious. There are numerous sub-specialties within this practice area.

Litigation - General Civil 1/2/3 √

Litigation is an impossibly broad categorization of practice area that encompasses any dispute between private parties (thus excluding government investigations). These disputes take place in a variety of forums including arbitration and other alternative dispute resolution methods as well as public litigation in state or federal court. Litigation is both the most crucial practice area to some of the most prestigious firms in the world as well as, perhaps, the practice area most available to the broadest set of law students, including those who did relatively poorly in a non-elite law school, because it is the practice area most commonly practiced by solo practitioners and smaller firms. Billing rates are similarly all over the spectrum, depending on the importance of the litigation matter, the client involved, and the amount at stake, among other factors.

Mergers and Acquisitions 1

Mergers and acquisitions is perhaps the most important practice area to the largest amount of large law firms. This practice area requires a large amount of associates and attorneys from specialist practice areas for law firms to bill out, and involves transactions that are always extremely important to clients and frequently involve large amounts of money. Such transactions, thus, universally receive very high billing rates. Working as an attorney in this space will involve equal amounts of advisory and transactional documentation work. In addition, you will serve as a quarterback in receiving and relaying advice from various specialist practice groups at the firm that are frequently involved in such transactions, as a large M&A deal may involve attorneys from the antitrust, securities law advisory, ERISA, tax, litigation, real estate, environmental, and finance departments.

Personal Injury 4 √

This practice area is a subset within litigation involving lawsuits alleging damages to a person's health due to negligence on the part of an owner, medical malpractice or a variety of other claims. Plaintiffs' attorneys are generally solo practitioners or small firms and work on contingency, while defense firms are slightly bigger and bill by the hour but are still relatively small. Attorneys realize success in this field via attaining partnership or starting one's own firm. This practice area is generally not considered that complex or sophisticated but entrepreneur attorneys can make much more money than they could at a larger law firm. However, most do not reach that level of success and there are few exit opportunities.

Real Estate 1/2/3/4 √

Real estate lawyers represent buyers, sellers, and lenders with regard to real estate transactions. This practice area is divided into two main buckets - "dirt," work related to development transactions, and bank finance practice which concerns the financing of the developments. Real estate legal practice is cyclical based on the real estate market and will also depend on the market in the geographic area around the law firm and not just the national market. Real estate practice ranges in complexity, prestige, and billing rates, based on how complex the transaction is, how much it is worth, and who the client is. Thus, working as a "real estate lawyer" ranges from commercial real estate development work, which is highly profitable and sought out by the most prestigious firms in the country, to residential real estate contracts for which in many cases attorneys charge fixed fees as low as $1000.

Securities / Capital Markets 1

Securities lawyers structure public and private debt offerings and public and private equity offerings in addition to advising on required securities filings, compliance with securities law and interacting with the Securities & Exchange Commission (SEC) and other regulators. This practice is both very steady and very profitable, as companies are always in need of additional capital, although public equity offerings have decreased in recent years. Securities lawyers tend to be known as somewhat more intellectual than attorneys in other areas of corporate practice due to the need for such attorneys to understand numerous technical provisions of federal securities law, rules, regulations, and formal and informal guidance from the SEC.

Sports / Entertainment / Media 3 N

These industries are combined not because entertainment and sports lawyers are interchangeable but because they advise their clients on similar contracts and it is equally difficult to obtain jobs in any of these niches. While attorneys in this field appreciate the opportunity to work for high-profile clients involved in transactions well-known to the public, these agreements are fairly simple and do not require nearly as much associate support as other areas of the law. There are some larger firms that engage in these practices but the practice groups are universally small; much of the work is performed by boutiques that again, while they may be prestigious, are relatively small. Do not stake your law degree on getting into this niche any more than you'd stake anything on becoming a sports professional, or you may be sorely (if unjustifiably, given the odds) disappointed.

Tax 1

Tax lawyers advise financial institutions, investors, corporations, and other businesses on how to structure transactions and their affairs generally in a tax-efficient manner. Clients may need or want tax lawyers to advise them on almost any type of transactions, and tax lawyers are indispensable to properly structuring such complex transactions as mergers and acquisitions, investment funds, and many securities offerings.

Tax law is among the most complex of any area of law due to the myriad number and complex nature of the laws, rules, regulations, cases, and formal and informal guidance undergirding federal taxation (some lawyers practice state and local tax, but most tax attorneys advise on federal taxation issues), and tax law is probably the area of law requiring the most knowledge of the law itself. Clients and attorneys in other departments frequently call on tax lawyers to invent creative structures to ensure that transactions are not considered taxable events and as a result, their advice needs to be accurate as it is frequently fundamental to the transactions at issue. Before deciding to become a tax lawyer, be sure to take tax classes in law school and try out assignments from a tax lawyer as a summer associate to ensure that you will be interested in the practice area and able to succeed.

Trusts & Estates 3 N

Trusts & estates law ("T&E") concerns the efforts of individuals to decide the future ownership of their assets and protect their assets in a tax-efficient manner; in some ways, T&E, like ERISA, is a subset of tax law.

While some law students are interested in T&E as they are under the impression that it allows a relatively stable work-life balance, entering T&E practice may be a career-limiting move. While many larger law firms have a T&E practice as a courtesy to clients and partners, these practices are generally very small and shrinking and generally not a profit engine for firms. T&E practice is quite specific and is not frequently exposed to corporate transactions like other areas of practice, and indeed even litigation attorneys frequently become more familiar with corporate practice than T&E lawyers. Moreover, the practice provides few lateral options - while there are boutiques that practice T&E, they will generally pay much less than the big firms as they do not have the other departments to subsidize the practice and clients tend to be not as ultra-high net worth as law firms, and there are very few in-house or governmental jobs in this area. As a result of all of these factors, think carefully before entering T&E practice if one of your goals is to be financially successful and you have other options.

Chapter 10: Types of Legal Employers

Many law students view the legal industry as an inscrutable mess of indistinguishably generalized lawyers making a lot of money and typing. As practicing lawyers understand, different employers and different areas of practice are fundamentally different from each other, and will present distinct paths to entry for law students. The below is an attempt to spell out these intricacies, by analyzing the various types of employers of entry-level lawyers.

Legal Services Jobs

1. Large Law Firm/Elite Boutiques

Barring a very strong connection and a resume that would otherwise have opened one up for an offer from OCI, it is likely a waste of time to reach out independently to large firms that are interviewing at OCI. It is possible to get an interview in the event you have a connection and/or a talent that is relevant to a particular practice area for which the firm is specifically in need of attorneys, but otherwise I wouldn't waste any time on such firms unless your next door neighbor is the hiring partner ... and you have dirt on him. Similarly, small but elite boutique law firms that exclusively hire alumni of large law firms or judicial clerkships are even more so a waste of time to engage with, as such firms generally don't hire any entry-level attorneys directly from law schools.

2. Small/Mid-size Law Firm

This is an enormous category of firms, as "small" and "mid-size" are vague terms that mean different things in different geographic areas. Ultimately, they share a common thread to the extent that such employers do not participate in OCI but are potentially interested in hiring entry-level attorneys. If you have good grades, these are a very good option simply given how many firms there are; 70% of attorneys in the private sector are employed at firms with less than 20 attorneys.[28]

As opposed to large law firms, which are largely national even if some of them only have a few offices, mid-size law firms are creatures of the geographic area in which they practice and generally only have one to a few offices. Thus, you need to mine your local legal magazines, directories, law school staff, and practitioners for information on such firms, and should avail yourself of the research methods discussed at the beginning of the chapter.

Connections are key to finding a job in this category barring truly impressive credentials. After learning about these opportunities, you need to figure out, hopefully, some connection to the firm to increase your chances, as any advertised openings at such firms will likely attract hundreds of responses. To be sure, however, if you can't find an opening, still apply. Moreover, with mid-size firms, if your grades are good it is not a waste of time to send in a resume even if the firm is not advertising an opening, if you have a connection.

Given how many firms there are within this category, the firms will be very different from one another. The salaries paid by and prestige of these firms vary wildly; some will pay less than salaries available to college graduates, while others will pay handsome six-figure salaries at a level close to their large law firm cousins. In addition, while jobs at high-end mid-size firms are generally secure for at least a couple of years, similar to their large law firm brethren, jobs with firms at the low end are extremely volatile and you may find yourself out of a job due to economic or other reasons with little prior warning. As a result, if you take a job at the low end of this spectrum, it certainly behooves you to never truly end your job search, but always keep an eye out and network even if relatively passively.

---

[28] https://www.law.georgetown.edu/careers/career-planning/private-sector-settings/small-medium-law-firms.cfm

3. Solo Practitioner

Working for a solo practitioner or a very small practice of less than 5 attorneys can provide an entry-level attorney with excellent front-row experience in practicing law, including courtroom experience and similar tasks that may take years to gain at other firms. However, there are also severe potential drawbacks to such opportunities. These jobs generally pay very little, the application process provides applicants with only a limited view of what the work environment will be like after being hired, and the position will not provide a meaningful credential on your resume. Ultimately, if you develop a strong connection with your boss and enjoy an entrepreneurial setting, it may be a good fit, but you may find yourself unable to find another job given the lack of prestige of the employer, or, even worse, looking for a new job relatively soon due to a lack of charisma between you and the boss.

A related option is to open one's own legal practice. At its most basic, this decision is essentially a decision to open a startup business. Just as with a startup, if you choose this option you will be responsible for all of the trappings of a business, be they marketing, real estate, cleaning the floor, payroll, bill collection, and, of course, performing the services, as well as complications unique to a legal practice such as malpractice insurance and client escrow accounts. While bar associations can provide mentoring and assistance, opening up a practice is overwhelmingly difficult for many new graduates due to all of these complications, let alone the extraordinarily difficult competition for business with the thousands of other, frequently more experienced practitioners.

4. Alternative Legal Services Provider

A wide variety of companies have emerged in recent years offering legal services in unique ways, for example, offering companies the ability to hire in-house help temporarily for particular projects, letting companies send repetitive documents to a central provider who will coordinate a response among solo practitioners, and a plethora of websites that help individuals and businesses locate qualified attorneys. If you find yourself with a lack of options or simply need a career change or greater flexibility, these companies may provide you income and experience without having to shoulder the burden of being a full-time employee or solo practitioner. However, many of these opportunities are only available to experienced attorneys with a good pedigree.

Government Jobs

1. Court System Attorney

Court systems need permanent law clerks and other staff to assist judges in researching cases and processing dockets. While salaries for these jobs are relatively low, they are generally higher than the low end of the small law firm market and also provide significant job security. However, the work may be more repetitive and boring than work at other employers, given that you will not be representing clients.

2. Federal Government Employee

There are two types of entry-level jobs in the federal government. First, there are "Honors Program" positions that are publicly announced; these positions are highly competitive and may be quite difficult to obtain for students who have not been able to obtain a summer associate position via OCI, except those with excellent grades. However, there are a variety of other entry-level attorney positions in various agencies in the federal government. Some are extremely competitive and are similarly low-likelihood for such students. For those jobs that are less competitive, some are publicly announced while others are not because attorney positions are excepted positions for which the usual civil service rules do not apply. The best route to these positions is either networking or interning for the agency. These methods can help you find out about non-public positions and position yourself at the top of the resume stack. Applying to public positions via the website will be a long process and you will be competing with hundreds and perhaps thousands of other applicants.

3. State / Local Prosecutor / Public Defender

These jobs may be available to a wider variety of candidates than federal jobs but provide a double whammy of low pay and stressful work that can take a significant emotional toll on you. You have to be able to sustain an aggressive persona and deal with emotionally charged issues on a daily basis. On the other hand, if you are interested in litigation, even outside of criminal law, this job will provide you priceless experience and will be secure. Despite the robustness of the experience you will gain, exit options, unless you rise significantly in seniority, will be much less lucrative than for federal prosecutors.

4. State / Local Regulatory Attorney

A wide variety of state and local regulatory bodies also need attorneys and some of these openings may be for entry-level positions. State legislators or legislative bodies also hire attorneys. The pay here will also be relatively low and will appeal to the more introverted personality that chafes at prosecuting criminals in open court.

Non-Profit Organizations

1. Public Legal Services Provider

These are jobs where you practice as a lawyer directly providing legal services to underprivileged individuals, such as at the Legal Aid Society. These jobs are very competitive, even though they pay relatively low salaries, because attorneys at these jobs receive a lot of responsibility and believe they are making a positive impact on the world. One of the best ways to obtain a job in this area is to intern for an employer in this field either during the summer and/or during the school year. If you impress the full-time attorneys during your internship you may be first in line if they have a new opening.

2. Public Interest Organization

There are many public interest organizations that do not, like legal services firms, actually provide legal services to underprivileged individuals, but rather provide advocacy for such populations or similar functions. These jobs are also extremely competitive and you will need to provide a significant demonstration of commitment, via prior work experience or other involvement, to the organization's cause. The pay will be relatively low and the job's security will depend on the continuing availability of funding, but many attorneys will find a significant amount of fulfillment from these jobs both in terms of what they accomplish as well as the lifestyle.

3. Legal Education / Administration

Every college needs pre-law advisors and there are a variety of administrative jobs within law schools, law firms, law firm clerk offices, law firm professional development offices, and law libraries that require a J.D. These jobs will generally pay more than state/local government jobs. However, they are career-limiting because you are ultimately not a practicing attorney nor will you be developing skills that will be helpful for practice in the future.

Corporate Jobs

1. In-House Attorney

While most in-house jobs are available only to practicing lawyers with several years of experience, several companies have opened programs to hire entry-level attorneys for lower-level legal work that they want to perform in-house to save money rather than sending to a law firm. These jobs frequently pay six-figure salaries or close to it and should be relatively secure as long as the need is there. Generally, there are no recruiters for these positions and, thus, you will have to wait until the company issues a public posting of the position. Of course, in such a case you should look to submit your applicant via a connection at the company. While internships may be a good way to develop a relationship with a company, this will only be available in the small minority of cases where the company that you are interning at has a job opening at the same time, and you should not give up summer jobs at employers that may hire you full-time for such a speculative situation.

2. Compliance

A variety of companies, most frequently financial institutions, recruit entry-level attorneys for compliance positions, where you will follow the firm's policies and procedures and ensure that the firm remains compliant with the rules and regulations of the regulatory bodies with jurisdiction over the firm. In these jobs, you will not be practicing as an attorney but holding such a position will leave open your ability to do so in the future if you switch to a position where you actually render legal advice regarding such rules and regulations.

3. J.D. Advantage Jobs

While many jobs will refuse to take resumes from someone who has a J.D., many other positions encourage but do not require a J.D.[29] While I subsume all such jobs within a single category, these jobs span a wide variety of industries and responsibilities, including corporate contracts administrator, alternative dispute resolution specialist, government regulatory analyst, legal editor or legal writer for legal or general newspapers and publications, professor, public affairs representative, risk manager, staff for politician or political campaign staffer, elected official, foreign service officer, and law enforcement / intelligence agent.

---

[29] See here for some initial discussion of these jobs from respected sources: http://www.nationaljurist.com/national-jurist-magazine/what-jd-advantage-career; http://www.nalp.org/jd_advantage_jobs_detail_may2013.

Legal Support Jobs

1. Legal Recruiter

From my anecdotal experience, almost all legal recruiters have J.D.s. I'm not sure why, as I don't know why candidates would care, but it may be that recruitment firms get so many resumes with J.D.s there is no reason to open it up to non-JDs. These jobs will pay okay. But having a job like this, even if you are an employee, is essentially like opening a business - if you are really good, you will do really well, even better perhaps than you would do at a large law firm. But if you are not successful, you will find yourself out of a job relatively quickly. For those with a personality that combines tenacity and exceptional people skills, it may be a great opportunity.

2. Document Review

In a document review position, attorneys continually review e-mails and other electronically stored documents for potential production in a litigation or governmental investigation to confirm whether the documents are responsive to the litigation's request, whether they are subject to the attorney-client privilege, and whether they contain noteworthy content. Many law students only turn to such positions out of sheer desperation after failing at all other options. There is a good reason for that attitude - these positions are incredibly dull. However, some law firms have permanent or semi-permanent positions in such a capacity that pay respectable full-time salaries, equivalent or higher to what many firms pay associates. While the work will be monotonous, at such a position you will gain a well-known name on your resume and exposure to high-profile matters, and I have seen junior attorneys use such a position to move to a job with which they are highly satisfied. On the other hand, working for document review agencies is both low-paying and frequently demeaning work, as working conditions may be poor and your schedule may be even more uncertain than associates at elite law firms.

3. Accounting or Litigation Consulting Firms

Both accountant and litigation consulting practices provide entry-level attorneys the ability to earn respectable salaries and develop skills in areas that are highly relevant to legal practice, although the attorneys will not technically be practicing law. These jobs leave open the possibility of making a significant income in the future as your expertise grows.

Major accounting firms recruit J.D.s for their tax divisions. At such a firm you will serve as a tax associate; while you could have obtained such a position with an accounting degree, your J.D. will provide you such opportunities even if you didn't obtain an accounting degree and will serve as a credential throughout your career, which in many cases involves lucrative positions such as law firm or accounting firm partner, in-house tax attorney or senior tax accountant positions at major corporations.

Litigation consulting firms analyze the facts involved in investigations and litigations. Given that these firms are called on to analyze complex issues in areas such as securities law, antitrust, or intellectual property, obtaining such a position will be easier if you have a degree and/ or relevant experience in technical areas such as the life sciences, computer science, or finance. You will become very familiar with how to conduct such investigations and will interact with attorneys at law firms and experts. As you grow more senior you may have the opportunity to develop an expertise in areas such as securities law or antitrust. If you get promoted within the firm, your pay may become quite lucrative as some litigation consulting firms have become extremely successful.

Chapter 11: Law Firm Taxidermy

Many law students and even junior lawyers do not understand how the legal industry is organized as an industry. Some hear vague terms such as "BigLaw," "mid-size" and "boutique" but do not appreciate on a substantive level - on a business level - how law firms distinguish themselves from each other. The below attempts, in a relatively summary fashion, to explain these differences by organizing law firms into various categories.

I. Large Law Firms

The "large law firm" industry is a highly competitive one. Participants in the industry run their organizations with pressures and benefits unique to not just the legal industry but to large law firms in particular. Before joining such an industry, is important to understand how the modern large law firm industry came to be, how it stands currently, and how different firms stand within it.

Prior to the mid-1970s and the 1980s, the large law firm industry was remarkably homogenous. Clients, even large institutions such as the large Wall Street investment banks, generally chose individual law firms for handling whole categories of legal work. Large law firms generally focused on a few core practice areas, such as corporate transactional work, mergers, securities law, and tax, and eschewed practice areas such as bankruptcy, real estate, and white collar crime. In addition, litigation was less important to most firms than it is today, simply because many attorneys counseled large companies to resolve their disputes outside of the courtroom. As is well known, prior to this period, many of the most prestigious firms first openly, and later more covertly, discriminated against women, religious, ethnic and racial minorities, and LGBT individuals.

Large firms at this time focused on prestige more than pure profit maximization. To be sure, law partners made a comfortable living, but partners, especially at the top firms, remained partners for life more frequently than today where partners must annually produce books of business to justify their compensation or risk being fired.

In the 1970s and 1980s, a band of upstart firms, such as Skadden Arps and Wachtell, sought out work in the practice areas that the large law firms had rejected, and began giving advice to clients on creative maneuvers both on the transactional and litigation side, such as engaging in hostile takeovers, aggressively defending against them, and using litigation affirmatively to enjoin corporate events or sue for alleged fraud. These firms rapidly grew. Clients started to more frequently divide up their legal matters among numerous law firms.

The large law firm industry became much more competitive. These dynamics were aided by increased transparency as to the profitability of law firms, a matter previously shrouded in complete secrecy. The American Lawyer, a new publication, began publishing figures in the 1980s on the total revenue each firm brought in. Even more controversially, it published the average "profits per partner," i.e. the bottom line income of the firm divided by the number of partners at the firm. That particular figure meant that not only did firms start actively and annually measuring their financial performance against each other, but partners became aware of how what they took home compared to the guy across the street - and the guy across the hallway.

This transparency and competition ushered in a new era. Partners increasingly looked to maximize their own yearly "profit," even if it meant moving firms to somewhere that was either doing better generally or was just willing to pay them more for the business the partner brought in. Law firms, keenly aware that their revenue producers might on any day not show up to work, looked to increase their total revenue and their profits per partner figures generally, and also shifted to a compensation model that more directly compensated based on books of business rather than seniority. While many firms initially resisted these trends, all but a negligibly tiny handful have now embraced it to varying degrees, especially after many firms that failed to remain profitable enough either collapsed completely or were swallowed up by other firms.

Today, large law firms grow on an amazingly consistent basis, with revenue and profits increasingly annually essentially without fail, a remarkable statistic for any industry. Of course, there is much noise behind the curtain, with some firms compensating rainmakers up to ten times more than other partners, and other firms largely serving as culture-less expense-sharing mechanisms for an army of solo practitioner partners. That being said, at the end of the day, law firms are a business, and their resilience speaks volumes to the hard work of law firm leaders in steering their firms through numerous headwinds, including the financial crisis and an explosion of alternative legal service providers.

A. The Elite

These firms are tied together by three threads: a. the high level of profitability for the partnership; b. the highly selective nature of the recruiting process; and c. the generally high-profile nature of the work these firms do and clients they represent. However, there are four sub-categories where their similarities break down.

1. Large Super Elite NYC-Based Firms

This category comprises a list of firms that is short enough to list comprehensively - Cravath Swaine & Moore, Sullivan & Cromwell, Davis Polk & Wardwell, Simpson Thacher & Bartlett, Paul Weiss Rifkind, Wharton & Garrison, Cleary Gottlieb Steen & Hamilton, and Debevoise & Plimpton. These eight firms are remarkably similar in many ways. All are based in New York City. All generally charge top of the market fees and thus generally only do work for clients with deep pockets and /or on matters that are extremely high profile and important, because those are the only clients and matters that can afford their fees.

Financially, all are in great shape. All rank near the top of rankings for profits per partner, ranging from $3 million per partner on the low end to over $6 million per partner on the high end. The financial crisis and ensuing shakeup of the legal industry only helped these firms, as many big corporations and financial institutions "fled to quality" and provided their high-value legal work to the most elite institutions to ensure nothing goes wrong. These firms rarely lose partners to other firms, a phenomenon due to both the enormously lucrative nature of practicing there, and the unusually collegial nature of these firms, which frequently divide up profits largely based on seniority instead of who is bringing in the business.

These firms are also remarkably similar in what they are not. None of them are among the industry's leaders in total revenue or attorney headcount. None of them provide a comprehensive suite of practice groups, instead focusing on high-value mergers and acquisitions, investment management, important civil litigation and white-collar investigations, and complex capital markets transactions, plus of course support departments like tax, ERISA, etc. These firms eschew building networks of far-flung offices all over the globe in favor of strategic placement of offices, generally in major financial centers.

In terms of recruiting, these firms are extraordinarily selective. Have a 3.5 from a top 10 law school and an excellent resume? Get in line. These firms look to hire the top of the class from the top law schools, and frequently hire more than half their summer associate class from the top five law schools. They will also hire from a range of other schools, and even occasionally from regional schools, especially those in New York City, but the competition will be extraordinarily fierce. That being said, these firms also hire upwards of 100 summer associates every year, due to high associate attrition and the large amount of work for junior associates given the large matters these firms handle.

Working as an associate at these firms is guaranteed to be intense. Due to their powerful reputations, they have no worry about attracting new talent, and as a result these firms churn through associates and give little regard, other than lip service, to retention. That may (or, rather, likely will) mean brutal conditions as an associate, depending on the practice area you are in and what is going on at the time. These firms similarly have fixed cultures, and will expect associates to adapt to them rather than the firm adapt to associates. This can be a good thing, in that a fixed culture means there are rules about how partners can treat you, but it also means that if you don't fit in, that is a greater problem than at a firm that is just a lot of partners sharing office space.

The quality of work available for junior associates is on par and at times better than similarly large but less elite firms. In terms of the quality of the level of responsibility, many to most of these firms will provide just as good level of responsibility as other larger firms - that is to say, erratic at best, and low-level at worst. The point is that you will not suffer from lack of on-the-ground experience from going to an elite large firm over another large firm. Indeed, at times, the frenetic pace of these firms create opportunities for some junior associates to get responsibility far beyond their years, but such opportunities will again be erratic and depend on equal levels of luck and pluck.

Working at these types of firms will also provide several benefits to a future career outside of the firm. On a most basic level, getting in at these firms provide you a life-long gold star on your resume. The nature of these firms' clients and matters ensures that the work will generally be high-profile and high-value, which equally enhances one's resume.

One final note that distinguishes these firms from all others. Financial institutions, governments, and corporations eagerly recruit associates at these firms. In particular, starting at these firms is the best chance you have of switching to a career on the business side of finance as an investment banker or similar.

2. Super Large Semi-Elite Firms

There are also several firms only slightly different than the above firms - namely, Skadden Arps Meagher Slate & Flom, Latham & Watkins, Kirkland & Ellis, Gibson Dunn & Crutcher, Weil Gotshal & Manges, Covington & Burlington, and Sidley Austin.

These firms are different in two aspects from the first category noted above. First, the recruiting requirements of these firms are somewhat more relaxed; these firms recruit from a wider variety of schools and level of class rank than the super elite firms noted above, and also seek lateral associates much more frequently than the firms noted above. Second, these firms do not, like the above firms, artificially limit their growth in terms of attorney headcount and offices like the super-elite. This means that these firms have more comprehensive practice areas. This will provide opportunities for associates who are interested in practice areas other than the fairly specific ones practiced by the super-elite firm. These firms also are more likely to compensate partners largely based on books of business.

Despite these differences, these firms are still largely similar to the most elite firms in the high-profile nature of the work and the dynamics created through extremely large annual incoming associate classes.

3. Big Elite Boutiques

The third type of "elite" firm consists of relatively large firms that focus on a narrow set of practice areas. Wachtell Lipton Rosen & Katz, Quinn Emanuel, Boies Schiller, Williams & Connolly, Munger Tolles & Olson, Irell & Manella, Susman Godfrey, and Kellogg Hansen Todd Figel & Frederick are all examples of this type of firm. These firms are very focused on what they want to accomplish. Most of them only have a small handful of offices and some (Wachtell, Williams & Connolly, and Kellogg Hansen) serve clients out of a single office. Several focus exclusively on litigation and investigations, while Wachtell advises on both transactional and litigation matter but due to its unique non-hourly billing system attracts only the truly crucial matters. These firms grow their attorney headcount very slowly, and have very small incoming associate classes, but due to the high-value nature of the matters they work on, are still extraordinarily profitable. The one firm on the above list that has not limited its growth in attorney headcount is Quinn Emanuel, which is included in this list as it focuses exclusively on litigation but has grown to over 700 attorneys.

In several ways, these firms are concentrated or super-charged forms of the other elite firms. These firms are not just as selective but more selective than the firms in the two categories noted above, as they require top credentials, class rank, and even sometimes a federal clerkship to be considered for even an interview. These firms also work their associates extraordinarily hard. However, in return, partnership may be somewhat easier to obtain due to the smaller associate classes and the decision by these firms to generally eschew recruiting established partners from outside the firm.

4. Small Elite Boutiques

There are also many boutiques, particularly in large urban centers, that are extremely selective in terms of what associates they will recruit, but have remained small - i.e. less than 50 attorneys.

These firms are "elite" in two ways. First, they handle high-profile matters that do not require an army of associates to complete, or work as co-counsel with big firms. Second, these boutiques only hire associates who have previously worked at a big firm or the government or at least have a federal clerkship, in addition to having outstanding academic credentials. They generally pay associates salaries that are comparable to those paid by large firms. However, while these firms are generally too small to make the cut of publishing profitability figures in The American Lawyer magazine, and thus their profitability is not publicly known, it can be safely assumed that, given their smaller size, partners in these firms make less than partners at large elite law firms.

The experience of associates and even partners at these boutiques - including the nature of the work they do, how hard they work, how collegial the atmosphere is, how safe the job is and how narrow the chances of joining the partnership - will be shaped by the unique personalities of the managing partners. While many attorneys have idealized views of these institutions, a leading recruiter has comprehensively explained that moving from a large firm to a boutique presents many dangers to a young attorney's career that need to be considered, in particular the personality-driven nature of these firms.[30] In short, while you may have more substantive responsibility at these firms, the culture may be more rough and uneven, you may have less professional resources than at a large firm, and you have a greater chance of being fired summarily with less exit options and worse treatment than you would receive at a large firm.

B. The Behemoths

There are many large law firms that have decided that the best strategy for their business is attaining the largest size in terms of attorney headcount and offices. These firms each arrived at this strategy after realizing that they were sandwiched in-between elite firms - who attract the best talent, sky-high rates, and are go-to for high-profile matters - on the one hand, and boutiques and other nimble mid-size or other smaller firms on the other, that have less infrastructure to support and can handle smaller matters for a range of clients for bargain rates. A law firm consultant, Bruce MacEwan, has dubbed firms that have found themselves sandwiched in this way the "hollow middle." Especially after the financial crisis in 2008, clients that previously funneled work to a small set of large law firms increasingly divided their matters into two piles, with the truly high-value work going to elite players and the commoditized work going to inexpensive nimble firms, with non-elite large firms left with little to stand on to compete.

These law firms have decided that the best way to compete is to be truly comprehensive, and have offices in every major place of business for their clients and offering a truly broad range of practice areas and expertise. These firms all have thousands of attorneys, and many of them attained such an amazingly large capacity through merging with other law firms, including other large law firms.

At many of these firms, associates and partners are divided into particularly small sub-practice areas. Instead of generally practicing litigation and

---

[30] http://www.bcgsearch.com/article/900047834/20-Reasons-Why-There-Is-No-Such-Thing-as-a-Lifestyle-Law-Firm-and-Why-You-Should-Beware-Moving-from-a-Large-Law-Firm-to-a-Boutique-Law-Firm/

investigations, associates at many of these firms will only work in civil litigation or only white collar investigations; indeed, at some associates will be pigeonholed even more narrowly on an informal basis, working with a small group of partners in a niche area. This is a natural aspect of partners providing themselves a protective group of associates and fellow-minded partners within the massive scope of these firms. How you are treated, how much work you have and your career trajectory will depend on your protective circle - and in turn their relative power - more than any fundamental culture or business direction of the firm generally.

Below I divide these firms into two categories - "mid-prestige" and "non-elite." Mid-prestige firms attract somewhat higher-profile work than the ones listed in the non-elite category and attract more highly credentialed junior associate candidates.

1. Super Large Mid-Prestige Global Firms

This category includes firms such as White & Case, Hogan Lovells, Mayer Brown, Clifford Chance, Linklaters, Allen & Overy, and Morgan Lewis.

2. Super Large Non-Elite Global Firms

This category includes firms such as Baker McKenzie, DLA Piper, Dentons, Norton Rose Fulbright, Squire Patton Boggs, Jones Day, Eversheds Sutherland, and Bryan Cave.

C. US-based Large Firms

Not all "sandwiched" firms have chosen "bigger is better" as their mantra. Others have grown to between 500 and 1,000 lawyers. These firms open overseas offices but remain based in the US, generally choose not to merge with European firms or other large US firms, and grow organically and strategically by adding lateral partners or small practice groups as needed. These firms, like their behemoth cousins, also make sure to "trim the fat" of partners that are not generating enough revenue.

1. Mid-Prestige Non-NYC-Based US-Centered Firms

The "mid-prestige" moniker represents that these firms remain highly sought out by highly credentialed law students and government attorneys, and frequently represent important financial institutions and corporations in high profile matters. Many of these firms have retained a unique culture, in part because these firms frequently remain controlled by attorneys in the region where the firm originated before it expanded across the country. These firms are generally highly profitable, if somewhat less than their elite law firm brethren.

This category includes firms such as Ropes & Gray, Paul Hastings, WilmerHale, Morrison & Foerster, O'Melveny & Myers, Akin Gump, Arnold Porter Kaye Scholer, Winston & Strawn, Goodwin Procter, and Dechert.

2. NYC-Based Profit Centers

These firms are all based in New York City. While they generally do not command the attention of the most highly credentialed law school graduates, these firms have succeeded in establishing themselves as a go-to destination for certain highly complex legal work, and in attracting a client base of financial institutions and other companies that regularly feeds them such highly profitable work. As a result, these firms enjoy profitability on a level comparable to the more elite firms. While each is known for particular niches, these firms all are generalists that also provide clients services in a broad array of transactional and litigation practice areas.

This category includes firms such as Cahill Gordon & Reindel, Schulte Roth & Zabel, Cadwalader, Wickersham & Taft, Fried Frank, Willkie Farr & Gallagher, Milbank Tweed Hadley & McCloy, and Shearman & Sterling.

3. Large Generalist US-Centered Firms

These firms were all previously focused on a particular region, but in the past few decades have expanded across the country. Their expansion certainly always includes New York City, but which other cities they expanded into will depend on the partner groups they were able to attract and the unique specialties and regional area that each firm originated with. While each of these firms are large in terms of attorney head count and number of offices, they are still much more well-known and enjoy a better reputation in the region where they originated than in other parts of the country. In addition, while each will stress that they are generalist firms that offer a comprehensive suite of services to a variety of industries, many of them continue to have much better reputations in particular practice areas or industry groups than in others.

This category includes firms such as Baker Botts, Foley & Lardner, Greenberg Traurig, Perkins Coie, Alston & Bird, Pillsbury, Vinson & Elkins, Holland & Knight, Baker Hostetler, Fox Rothschild, K&L Gates, Hunton & Williams, Nixon Peabody, King & Spalding, and Orrick, Herrington & Sutcliffe.

4. Large US-Centered Firms with Unique Focus

These firms have hundreds of lawyers, numerous offices, and a full suite of practice areas, but are less abashed about emphasizing their strengths in particular practice areas or industry groups. For example, in terms of practice areas, McDermott remains particularly strong in health law and trusts and estates, Proskauer Rose has strengths in sports law and intellectual property, and Jenner is a powerhouse in litigation, while Wilson Sonsini and Cooley actively courts clients in their wheelhouse of venture capitalist and technology companies. The work these firms do is frequently high-value and the clients are frequently very successful, permitting these firms to grow into other areas.

This category includes firms such as Wilson Sonsini, McDermott Will & Emery, Proskauer Rose, Cooley, and Jenner & Block.

5. Large Firms Specializing in Commodity Work

These firms are large in terms of attorney headcount and number of offices, but focus on a particular practice area or areas. In addition, the practice areas these firms practice have become more commoditized over time, as clients don't view these deals or litigation as presenting important risks. As a result, these firms charge much lower billing rates and are much less profitable than other large corporate law firms.

Firms in this category include Jackson Lewis, Littler Mendelson, Wilson Elser, and Hinshaw & Culbertson.

II. Large-End Mid-Size Firms

This category is of firms that still attract business from large corporations and significant attention from top-50 law students and lateral associates from big firms. What makes mid-size firms different? Most will "only" have a few hundred lawyers, as opposed to many of the firms above which will have close to or over 1,000 attorneys. However, the distinguishing of the "mid-size" label from "large law firms" is not just in the number of lawyers - Wachtell also has less than 300 lawyers, and many firms that I list below have more than the ones I list above.

The keyword is "less." Mid-size firms attract less of a lot of things than large firms - the firms are generally smaller, with firms with larger headcount spread across numerous offices with no particularly large offices, the matters are less high-profile and less complex, the matters require less associates per case and as a result partner associate ratios are smaller, billing rates are lower and margins and profits are compressed, and these firms generally attract candidates from lesser-known law schools or lateral partners from lesser-known firms. One other distinction from large firms is that these firms generally focus on the domestic market, with at most a couple of overseas offices.

These firms are also businesses but do not include some of the extremes of the big firms. They will seek, like their larger brethren, to reward top performers, but it will be the rare firm that will compensate one partner ten times more than another, given that there is no army of associates at these firms to provide the cushion for the big paydays of the rainmakers and no mountain of constantly incoming new matters to provide work for service partners. Instead, underperforming partners will simply be asked to leave rather than a rainmaker receiving many times more compensation than a service provider. Ultimately, these firms are no happy go lucky paradise, but the fighting over money is somewhat narrower than at larger firms.

These firms can be further divided into three categories. The first type of firm provides a comprehensive suite of practice areas and a national footprint of offices. The second group of firms are generalists but have remained focused on a particular region while expanding into various other cities nationwide. Firms in the third category focus on or are known for a particular niche or specialty even if they also have relatively small general practice groups.

1. Mid-Size Generalist National Firms

This category includes firms such as Blank Rome, Duane Morris, Sheppard Mullin, and Locke Lord.

2. Mid-Size Generalist Regional Firms

This category includes firms such as Kramer Levin, Troutman Sanders, Davis Wright Tremaine, Ballard Spahr, Kilpatrick Townsend & Stockton, HaynesBoone, Fenwick & West, McGuire Woods, Pepper Hamilton, and Venable.

3. Mid-Size Specialist Firms

This category includes firms such as Kasowitz Benson, Drinker Biddle & Reath, Arent Fox, Steptoe & Johnson, Mintz Levin, Crowell & Moring, Fish & Richardson, and Hughes Hubbard & Reed.

III. Small-End Mid-Size Firms

These firms - which generally have 150 to 300 attorneys - are fundamentally different than any of the above firms in that most of them do not compete for revenues from large corporations or large financial institutions. While large or companies that are located near these firms may provide some business to these firms, these companies look to a broader base of types of clients, including a range of businesses, for-profit and non-for-profit institutions, and individuals. Those matters that larger institutions do provide these firms will frequently involve much smaller dollar amounts and complexity than matters provided to bigger firms. These firms, especially since the financial crisis, have found themselves both unable to obtain the complex, high-value work that feeds the large law firm profit machines, and unable to charge rates on truly commoditized work sufficiently high to pay partners and associates competitive compensation.

As a result of these pressures, firms at this level tend to be more focused than large law firms and larger mid-size firms in one or more ways. Many of them have remained within a single region of the country, such as the East Coast, Southeast or Mountain West. While some are generalists, many remain focused on a set of specific practice areas rather than promising proficiencies in every major transactional and litigation matter for big corporations and financial institutions, with some focusing on particular niches - such as environmental law, unique regulatory issues, or first amendment issues - that most big firms avoid completely or do not focus on.

A good way to identify these firms is by reading a report by the American Lawyer publication called the "AmLaw 200," which is a ranking of the top 200 law firms in the country with the highest revenue. The firms listed in the second hundred spots on this list are a good proxy for small-end mid-size firms, although some firms will belong to the category of "elite boutiques" noted above.

IV. Small Firms

Despite the buzz attracted by large and mid-size firms, most attorneys in this country work at small law firms of 50 attorneys or less. Indeed, the problem with providing meaningful feedback about these firms as a category is precisely because there are so many of them.

What can be said is that each of these firms are shaped by the unique personalities of the firm's partners, the practice areas it practices, and the type of clients and geography it serves. These firms will generally not provide a full suite of practice areas for large corporations, although they can attract business from local corporations and financial institutions regarding matters that are not highly complex or labor-intensive. Nor will they venture beyond a single geographic region or even frequently a single metropolitan area, with most sporting a single office. In addition, as opposed to attorneys at large and mid-size firms which almost unanimously specialize in a single practice area, many of these firms will have attorneys serve as generalists or focus on multiple practice areas to spread resources efficiently.

For attorneys, this disparity also means that compensation is a black box that is specific to the firm and individual in question. Large law firms across the country pay identical rates to associates; while some small firms will pay relatively close to those rates, very few will match and most will provide only a small fraction of such compensation. In addition, the compensation of partners at these firms will also be highly variable, with many partners at these firms making less than associates at large and mid-size firms.

Ultimately, a small firm is a more entrepreneurial form of law firm that provides flexibility in structure but can still provide an extremely fulfilling career. Attorneys at smaller firms report higher job satisfaction than their colleagues at large firms, perhaps due to greater variety of the work, client contact or better work-life balance that many small firms provide. These firms can also compete with larger firms in name recognition, as many of these firms are highly regarded within that metropolitan area or region even as their name recognition does not travel far beyond those environs.

Firms of this type can be divided into small commercial firms that service mid-size and small businesses and institutions, small general firms that service both individuals and businesses, and solo practitioners. There are far too many to list.

Chapter 12: Inside a Modern Law Firm

The law firm is a world unto itself, filled with a wide variety of personalities, idiosyncrasies and delicate political situations. There is good reason for this: Law firms regularly manage some of the most sensitive problems affecting the most important corporations and financial institutions in the world. Law practice is big business for law firms, many of which earn hundreds of millions to billions of dollars of revenue every year. The legal work performed by lawyers is highly important to clients, whether big or small. Thus lawyers rightly take seriously both their own job and their general work environment.

It is critical to enter a law firm with a clear understanding of what goes on inside and realistic expectations about your role. Simply getting a job and assuming you will just work hard and hopefully succeed is a recipe not just for failure but suffering, pain, frustration, excessive stress and shattered expectations. Careers are ruined prematurely and unnecessarily.

It is the goal of this chapter to provide a run-down of the various categories of "players" within a law firm. The chapter will explain the role of each category within the law firm generally as well as provide strategies as to how a new associate should relate to these types of people to maximize the junior associate's potential success.

1. Managing Partner / Management Committee

At the top of the law firm food chain is the managing partner, CEO, or Management Committee. These partners are literally running the law firm. Sometimes in consultation with the broader partnership, firm management makes fundamental decisions regarding the firm's strategy, such as which lateral partners to bring in and which partners to let go. These are important people.

Nevertheless, don't worry for now about getting on their good side. There are so many levels between who you need to impress and this crew, the best strategy is to just stay out of their radar and avoid annoying them.

2. Equity Partner / Shareholder

Equity partners are the type of people at a law firm most important for you to impress, perhaps unsurprisingly. But who are these people, and what is the mysterious "equity" word?

A brief explanation of the basic corporate underpinnings of the modern law firm enterprise is necessary before answering this question. A law firm is a partnership, which is a legal form of organizing a business enterprise whereby the enterprise is owned by partners. The "partnership" is an ephemeral item that automatically "passes through" all of the profits or losses of the enterprise to the individual partners - the partnership's owners. This is opposed to a corporation, which is a separate legal entity that counts its own income and pays its own taxes, is managed by a board of directors, and only passes through profits if dividends to shareholders - the corporation's owners - are approved.

The law firm partnership is owned by the equity partners - and the equity partners alone. The percentage of "equity" - or ownership units - they possess will directly determine how much money they make. The reason why "equity partner" doesn't just translate to "partner" is because in many modern law firm, many if not most partners are not "equity partners." Rather, they have only been given the title partner, but are paid compensation based on a salary and bonus, largely identical to how associates are paid except that instead of standard compensation for all members of a certain class year, individual partners are compensated individually.

Law firms have also made it increasingly difficult in recent decades to attain partner status. Previously, large law firms exclusively named new partners out of their upcoming associates, and named partners regularly to ensure the growth of their business and incentivize associates. After the corporatization of large law firms that occurred from the 1980s through the financial crisis, law firms made several interconnected decisions modifying how they grow. First, they increased their partner/associate ratio and the "leverage" they use to make money from client accounts. As partners supported more and more furiously billing associates, law firms were able to increase profits without having to name new partners. This decrease in naming new partners in turn further increased the profits of each partner, as it took away the slices of the pie that the new partners would have taken away. Second, law firms increasingly turned to lateral partners with established books of business to support growth rather than taking chances on associates with no proven client development track record. Finally, firms took a stricter view that the naming of new partners is a step to be taken episodically only when absolutely necessary, rather than a fundamental aspect of the business model. These changes weren't all bad for associates - as associates came to terms with the decreasing potential for being named partner, they demanded higher compensation, which they received in 2001, 2006, 2007 and again in 2016.

How does one reach the exalted pedestal of partner today? Basically dumb luck. Barring bringing in $5 million a year in business, there is nothing you really can do to be named partner. Working crazy hard, being generally well liked, and praised by clients is just the beginning. It is also important to be working in a niche that is in high demand at the time you are being considered for partner, and to have worked on high-profile and /or high-importance matters that got you the attention of firm leaders and clients.

3. Rainmaker

One particular subset within the tent of equity partners is the semi-mythic rainmaker - the partner that brings in a meaningful amount of business. As presently most law firms demand that every partner originates (the law firm term for "bring in") business or else face eventual termination, the term rainmaker is reserved for those partners that bring in more business than necessary to pay for their compensation.

Rainmakers are very important people at law firms. They have considerable power vis-à-vis not just associates but also other partners. Even if multiple partners are working on the same matter, the rainmaker's view will usually win out and the other partners will (unless they are stupid) defer to him or her.[31]

Rainmakers will work with others at the firm in one of three ways depending on the political and financial structure of the firm in question. At the firms with the weakest cultures, rainmakers will attempt to assist their clients themselves or with small teams of associates and with the least possible consultation with other lawyers, in particular avoiding other partners and counsel. They will pursue this course to ensure that they are granted credit for the business origination and that others do not attempt to "steal" the client and claim credit for its business or a portion thereof. At other firms (the prevalent model at many and perhaps most firms), rainmakers will develop "teams" of partners, counsel and associates in various niches to assist them in counseling "their" clients on various issues. These teams may or may not work with other teams, depending on the firm in question and the importance of the issue. At other firms, a small minority of firms, generally skewing towards the highly elite firms with extremely healthy profits, partners work together and help out on client work essentially as needed dependent on the expertise necessary and availability.

It is important for associates to pay attention to which of the partners bring in business, but not in the way one might think. Attempting to in any obvious way "kiss up" to rainmakers or attempt to work directly for them while one is still a junior associate will usually not work, as rainmakers usually don't deal directly with junior associates. Indeed, deliberate attempts can seriously backfire as the associate may give the impression of not being a team player. To be sure, there are junior associates that will attract the attention of important partners and will work directly with them and attain

---

[31] A side issue is whether this is good for clients or not, given that there is no necessary correlation between a lawyer's business generation skills and their legal skills.

responsibility and client contact beyond what is typical for others at their level. However, those associates are rare, they frequently have unique skill sets in terms of personality, and such situations usually arise because the partner notices the associate rather than due to any deliberate plan on the associate's part.

Instead of obvious attempts to work with rainmakers, associates should pay attention to the structure of the "teams" existing at the firm in question and attempt to get involved in a team of a rainmaker who is involved in types of matters or clients in which the associate is interested. Associates should seek out work from a rainmaker's "deputy" or "grand deputy," the service partners or senior associates that work on the rainmaker's teams. Associates should look to develop relationships with the deputies even when the deputies happen to be working for another partner or on another type of matter. Once the associate has a relationship with that person, the associate may receive work from the rainmaker's matters as well when the grand deputy needs "another body" on one of those matters. With such an approach, if the associate does good work and is otherwise a good member of the team, the associate will be able to develop a relationship with the rainmaker in a natural and organically growing manner.

4. Service / Non-Equity Partner

As noted above, law firms have become much more careful in giving out equity to new partners, and a large percentage of the partnership in many law firms are non-equity partners. These partners are compensated at a level that is frequently only slightly higher than that of senior associates and counsel, and work on matters assigned to them by rainmaker partners in a manner somewhat similar to how to work is assigned to associates. Service partners may have no business of their own, have some but not enough to work exclusively on their own matters, or in some cases do have business but are asked to work on a matter for another partner due to their special expertise.

While service partners may not have a base of power accruing from business generation, they are still the leader of the deal or litigation teams that they oversee. When rainmaker partners ask service partners to run a matter for them and their client, the rainmaker frequently delegates significant authority and discretion over the matter to the service partner. Politically, the service provider will preside over team meetings and will frequently be the only partner that associates have contact with, as the service partner in many cases will update the rainmaker privately on an as-needed basis regarding important issues. In some matters, the rainmaker will only get involved in the matter when it reaches a truly important stage, at which point the rainmaker will assume control over day-to-day issues from the service partner.

Ultimately, however, service partners will generally have discretion regarding the number and identity of associates on a team and who does what. As a result, associates should make sure to treat service partners with the respect accruing to a team leader. At times, a rainmaker may task a senior associate or counsel with certain workstreams related to a matter outside of the purview of the service partner, but even in such cases, impressions should be actively managed - woe to the associate that gives the impression that he or she is disloyal to the service partner.

5. Retired Partner

Rounding out the partner ranks are the retired partners. These are partners that have retired from working on client work on a regular basis. At many firms, all partners - even rainmakers - are required to retire at an age certain, 65 or 70, for instance. Other firms make certain exceptions for truly important individuals. Firms require retirement to ensure that partners duly pass on client relationships to the next generation and help ensure the continuity of the firm. Many firms provide retired partners with pensions that are quite generous - hundreds of thousands of dollars per year. Others also provide them with access to an office and a secretary. Retired partners may work on your matters from time to time but are generally not involved except on extraordinary matters or in client relations on a high level.

6. Counsel / Senior Attorney / Senior Counsel / Of Counsel

Many firms have an attorney position, dubbed as "counsel," "of counsel," "senior counsel," or "senior attorney," based on the firm, that is defined by what it is not. A counsel on the one hand usually does not have power or discretion over client matters like a partner, and does not get paid or treated like a leader of the law firm that a partner is. On the other hand, they are not associates that are loosely "associated" with a law firm, but instead have a fixed position. Counsel are generally provided one of three types of work by partners - supervision over teams on relatively minor transactions or litigation matters, requests for the counsel's view on complex matters of law that the counsel has developed an expertise in, and completion of one-off projects.

The counsel position is a window into how modern law firms operate. Typically, a law firm names someone as counsel when the law firm values their work but does not believe the attorney has supervisory or business development capability sufficient to justify making him or her partner. The other instance where law firms will make someone counsel is if they want to hire a senior attorney from the government or another firm, but want to test out the attorney before naming him or her as a partner. As large law firms have reduced the relative percentage of associates that they name as partners, they have increased the amount of counsels to ensure that client work is completed.

Law firms treat counsel differently in multiple ways. With regard to compensation, while compensation for associates in many large law firms is fixed based on class year, counsel compensation is largely discretionary. Counsel compensation will generally always be more than what senior associates receive, and counsels in major firms can make $500,000 in total compensation. A counsel's job security is also unique - generally tied to the amount of available work in the counsel's niche. A counsel position is not, any more than anything else at a law firm, set for life, but generally once an associate is named counsel the job is safe for at least a few years, barring an enormous drop in available work. Indeed, counsel may have more job security than partners, who are expected to generate business.

The relatively large amount of compensation counsel receive is in return for the relative lack of importance of the counsel within the organization, a phenomenon keenly observed by both partners and associates. At many firms, a firm naming an attorney as counsel means that the firm has made an essentially final judgment that the individual will never be named partner. As a result, counsel in some cases have less power and authority than even senior associates that still could potentially make partner. In many cases they are not given supervisory authority over associates, and even when they are delegated such authority, the above dynamic can make asserting the authority difficult. It is due to complications such as these that in many firms, more counsel are named in niche departments such as tax and ERISA that advise on a particular area of law rather than supervise large deal teams and thus lend themselves to counsels providing advice individually.

The true authority of a counsel is ultimately a question dependent on the individual circumstances and should be approached as such. Counsel in many cases do have significant authority and, especially given that they may have been scarred by attempts to subvert their authority, may impose it harshly at times. Associates should thus be wary of ever defying a counsel. Counsel also may have very strong relationships with certain partners. On the other hand, counsel can serve as competitors to service partners when they are delegated with authority by a rainmaker partner, and thus associates should make sure to not be overly deferential to the counsel in such circumstances. Ultimately, working with counsel is something a junior associate should approach carefully.

7. Senior Associate

The title senior associate is generally applied to associates who have been working as a lawyer for more than five years. Senior associates are strategically important for law firms. Senior associates in many cases run day-to-day operations of deal or case teams, at times even the most important matters. Senior associates are responsible for, *inter alia*,[32] distributing tasks to mid-level and junior associates, serving as the face of the team with clients, service providers, and law firms representing other companies in the same deal or litigation, and of course working with more senior members of the team, be they rainmakers, service partners or counsel.

Working as a senior associate is an incredibly fraught and straining job. Any time savings provide by the ability to delegate tasks to junior associates is swallowed up and then some by the crush of emails, phone calls, and meetings with all of the parties noted above. That work alone is the equivalent of a full-time job, but senior associates must also carefully review all of the work delegated to junior and mid-level attorneys, and perform themselves any high-level tasks requiring great expertise. If they want to be considered for advancement, senior associates cannot be content with just staying above water with day-to-day tasks like a junior associate. Instead, they must think strategically about the matter, a task that frequently involves weighing options with no absolute "best answer" and creatively identifying the best approach for the client even outside of what appears in the precedent or research. Politically, senior associates must contend with junior and mid-level attorneys who may be extremely competitive and attempt to elbow the senior associate out of a supervisory role, manage their relationships with partners and counsel, and establish themselves as someone who is at once a forceful and effective leader and also someone sufficiently fair that junior associates enjoy (or at least tolerate) working for.

Senior associates also face a crossroads in their career unlike those faced by other lawyers. On the one hand, even the fact that an attorney has survived at a large firm long enough to be a senior associate is an accomplishment and exciting event. At many law firms, most associates leave within five years, and at some, most leave in the first few years. An associate remaining at a law firm for six or seven years means that the firm has a high regard for the associate. Serving as a senior associate is also exciting for an attorney

---

[32] Look it up!

because it is the first time for many that the attorney will be able to work in a true supervisory capacity over important matters after years of toiling late night after late night on relatively simplistic tasks. Senior associates have proven the quality of their work, and law firms need such quality attorneys to supervise their matters and thus look to ensure retention of senior associates.

On the other hand, continuing on as a senior associate carries potential danger to the associate's career. Mid-level attorneys have many career options - moving in-house to a position at a corporation or financial institution, clinching a government position, or, most frequently, moving to another firm at which the associate believes there are greater long-term prospects as a partner or counsel. As one grows more senior, those options decrease. In-house employers may view a super-senior associate as overqualified, and law firms may not want to pay the large salaries that senior associates command. Nor will law firms necessarily allow the senior associate to move down in class year and accept a lower salary as they will believe that the senior associate will grow unhappy with reporting to people with less experience.

Serving as a senior associate is thus in effect a commitment to the associate's current law firm. If the law firm makes the associates partner or counsel, that commitment will have paid off, but if the law firm informs the associate in a few years that they should find another job or simply fires the associate, the commitment may have been ill-advised.

Due to these risks, associates owe it to themselves to make continuing on as a senior associate a conscious decision with a full appreciation with the attendant risks and reward, and avoid simply doing so out of inertia or because of clouded judgment due to the exciting prospect of supervisory authority. Each associate at this stage in a career should assess what the associate's career goals are, and whether the current law firm has a realistic shot of fulfilling them. Law firms, for their part, are quite clear that there is no reason for associates to assume they have long-term job security. Law firms are businesses, and exclusively look out for their own interests, not those of associates, and they are not going to give up on the assistance that senior associates provide to help an associate's career, nor are they going to clog up the ranks of partners and counsel when it strategically does not make sense. Unfortunately, some associates simply ignore the explicit and implicit messages that firms broadcast to associates generally and to individual associates in formal and informal reviews; make sure you do not make that mistake.

What can a senior associate do to advance in the firm? Beyond truly excelling at people management and communication skills with a variety of parties inside and outside the firm, and displaying creativity, extraordinary diligence, and outstanding legal acumen, client contact is critical to a senior associate. Senior associates should ensure that they are well-liked by clients and work on high-profile matters. If clients are telling firm management that a particular senior associate is excellent, the law firm will listen, and the opposite is certainly also true.[33]

8. Mid-Level Associate

Mid-levels are the sandwich generation of a large law firm. This group, which is generally assumed to contain associates undergoing their third, fourth and fifth years of work after law school, no longer consists of immature, eager and unexperienced junior associates. They have experience in their niche and generally have (or should have) the ability to create complex legal documents and give fairly complex legal advice on certain topics. Given their increased level of sophistication as opposed to junior associates, law firms can safely entrust mid-levels with highly complex work, and as a result mid-levels frequently work extremely hard. On the other hand, mid-levels are frequently not delegated supervisory authority over an entire deal or case team like senior associates, and of course receive smaller salaries than those associates. It is because of this mix of significant experience and relatively low cost that law firms find mid-level associates to

---

[33] This is contrast with junior associates; many junior associates seek out and are enlivened by client contact, but excellent relationships within the law firm at that stage is much more important than client contact outside the firm.

be the most important people in the law firm to retain, aside from rainmakers, of course.

There are three touchstones necessary to succeed as a mid-level associate - execution, execution, execution. A mid-level will be counted on by partners and senior associates to successfully complete a variety of legal tasks, be they drafting documents for a deal or preparing for depositions or drafting briefs on a litigation. A mid-level will have juniors to push the buttons, but they have to tell them which to push, how hard, and when - a mid-level can never expect anyone more junior than him or herself to execute judgment or possess expertise. The mid-level needs to think about where the junior associates could go wrong and carefully review their work, and contemplate what other parts are necessary to ensure that nothing is otherwise missing or problematic about the finished product. Every meeting should be comprehensively prepared for, every document a partner could want should be brought and every question should be anticipated. Finally, while a mid-level will not yet be making substantive decisions about a case, he or she should also display an interest and knack in contributing to such decisions and inspire trust that he or she could be delegated such issues in the future.

A junior associate will find that many of his or her tasks are supervised by mid-level associates. Senior associates will frequently farm out parts of large cases or deals to mid-levels to handle with the assistance of junior associates. As such, and especially near the beginning of a new associate's tenure at the firm, a junior associate may find him or herself in most cases working directly with mid-level associates much of the time.

It is thus very important for junior associates make sure to develop close professional relationships with mid-level associates. In essence, junior associates should "develop" mid-level associates as sources of work, billable hours, and assignments related to clients, types of legal matters, and industries in which the junior associate is interested, much of the same way a partner would "develop" a client for business generation. To be sure, all attorneys at a law firm should look to develop those with greater seniority than themselves in a similar way, but junior associates should perhaps focus on this group the most, given that junior associates do not yet have a base of experience and proven work ethic and results to offer like more senior attorneys do.

9. Junior Associate

Ah, junior associates - the proletariat of law firms. Junior associates have a wide variety of experiences at law firms, of course, but *ex ante* every junior associate should expect a wild ride. Junior associates are expected to be willing to do almost any type of work, to enter and exit deal and case teams as needed, to be willing to perform small isolated tasks for such teams without receiving transparency into the case as a whole, and be ready to work literally 24-7-365. Law firms, perhaps justifiably so, view these circumstances as simply the price of admission for the large compensation that junior associates receive, which at many firms is $180,000 plus bonus, despite a complete lack of experience. They also feel little incentive to avoid cranking up the heat, given that associates with less than two years of experience have few to no competitive exit options other than a judicial clerkship.

One pitfall for junior associates is an excess of ambition - juniors should be excited about their work but should display ambition only in a carefully cabined way. First, with regard to the type of tasks one wants to do, junior associates should be happy to do a variety of "low-level" tasks given that they do not have significant experience. There may indeed be times, such as where mid-level associates are not available or where a junior associate has impressed a partner or senior associate, where junior associates will be called upon to complete tasks or engage in supervision beyond what is typical, but a junior associate should not expect those opportunities or be overly eager to receive them. Given that junior associates do not in the majority of cases have the requisite experience, those more senior may view a junior's naked ambition as indicative of a lack of appreciation for the importance of the legal matter to the client, or simply overly aggressive. With regard to the type of matters as well, while junior associates should look to volunteer to work for partners or senior associates covering types of legal matters, clients or industries in which the junior associate is interested, junior associates should not expect at this stage to be given work exclusively in one particular area of interest. A junior is there to cover those issues that the firm needs them for and to gain basic legal skills, and explicitly asking for a different deal may again be seen as overreaching and immature.

Another aspect of this stage of a career that can be confusing to some is how to work most effectively with other junior associates. Large law firms are somewhat unique in that, as opposed to other types of service firms such as public accounting firms, in many instances multiple junior associates work on the same deal or case team, either at the same time or with different junior associates rotating in and out of the teams. Make no mistake about it - the other junior associates are competition. You should learn to form alliances with other associates, but that does not make them your friends. This effect is exacerbated because many lawyers are, unsurprisingly, highly competitive people who enjoy triumph over others even when the rewards, such as a slightly higher-profile assignment, are relatively minor.

Whether you identify with this competitive mindset or not, there are several points to keep in mind. If you are competitive, be careful to not overdo it. You will be working with your fellow junior associates both currently and throughout your career at the law firm, and will have to frequently collaborate with them. You will need their help at times and they will in turn seek you out for assistance as well. Reward those who help you out and avoid stabbing others in the back - it will come back to haunt you the next time you in turn need a bailout. Avoid giving the impression that you are overly competitive, as that will not be appreciated by senior attorneys who want a well-oiled machine for their deal or case teams with as little drama as possible.

For those who shy away from explicit competition, the environment of many large law firms may be emotionally trying, even traumatic. Ultimately, you have to realize that large law firms are executing high-profile legal work for large corporations and financial institutions, for which partners receive millions and you in turn are receiving a salary far beyond the dreams of most Americans. In an environment where so much is at stake, you will have to learn to be happy or at least tolerate dealing with highly competitive people. These people don't only work at your firm, they are at every type of firm, whether large or boutique, and also at that company or financial institution offering in-house gigs and at the government agencies offering legal positions. If you truly cannot bring yourself to stand working with ambitious and demanding people, frankly the legal profession may not be the best fit.

10. "The Others" - Staff Attorneys, Paralegals, Support Staff

At many firms, partners and partner-track associates only represent a slim majority of employees. To properly serve clients, law firms also need a variety of other professionals. This list includes staff attorneys, who are non-partner-track attorneys, typically without the pedigree demanded of associates, that handle repetitive tasks such as document review or focus on a single commoditized legal area, such as obtaining antitrust clearance for mergers and acquisitions. In addition, almost every law firm will have some secretarial coverage for partners and partner-track associates, although secretaries have decreased in number at large law firms due to increased automation. This group also includes paralegals, who are professionals, generally college graduates, that assist attorneys with tasks that are relatively administrative in nature and generally do not involve a high degree of discretion, but involve some thought and are thus inappropriate for secretaries. Other support staff perform a wide variety of functions including graphic design, reproduction and binding, e-discovery, document editing, securities filings, and managing electronic court filings.

For a junior associate, there are three points of advice common to working with all such professionals. First is to simply be aware of the extent of support available at one's law firm and what one can delegate to others. Frequently, juniors may toil all night on an assignment involving a large amount of administrative work that they could have delegated to a paralegal or document editor. Working with such staff is beneficial to everyone involved - it saves the client the higher billing rate that the associate would have charged, it provides the support staff with work, and gives the associate a couple of hours of sleep. Of course, in many such instances, the associates want the extra hours so that they can bill more, which is a separate issue, but assuming you are not hoarding hours, support staff may be a life-saver.

Second, and countervailingly, while you should feel more than free to delegate to such personnel, you cannot delegate responsibility over the quality of the product they produce and you send in turn to your supervisors. Partner-track attorneys, not support staff, are charged with exercising judgment, and in the view of clients and partners, it is your responsibility to review the work of support staff. No one will care about your excuses and any attempt to explain a mistake based on the work of support staff will only make you look worse than simply apologizing.

The third piece of advice is to treat every person at a law firm with basic human respect and decency. Too many attorneys become rude and short-tempered after working at a large law firm. One can be sympathetic to this phenomenon - it is in part the result of simply working extremely hard on extremely taxing issues under large amounts of stress due to the need to get everything perfect. In addition, in many instances, a junior associate may simply learn such behaviors by osmosis by how they in turn are treated by partners or senior associates. But sympathy does not equal justification. If you consider yourself a moral person, human decency should always be your touchstone. However badly you are treated, be the bigger person and don't simply pass the garbage down to your subordinate in turn. Outside of morality as well, if you treat others badly, you may develop a reputation which may negatively affect either how more senior attorneys view you or attempts by more junior personnel to avoid working with you. But even if there are no practical effects on your work, being nice and fair is simply the right thing to do.

Chapter 13: Succeeding as a Summer Associate

For those fortunate to have received an offer from OCI or otherwise to join the summer associate program at a large or mid-size law firm, save your self-congratulations - you are still 6-8 weeks away from receiving an offer to join the firm full-time as an associate. Law firms will only hand out those offers if you survive the summer associate program.

Thankfully, most summer associates receive offers at most firms[34]; at many of the most prestigious firms in recent years, 100% or close to 100% of summer associates generally receive offers to return to the firm full-time. However, you should definitely treat the program seriously; being no-offered will not only eliminate your future with the firm in particular but it may permanently impair your career prospects as other firms will also not want to hire you due to concerns as to why you did not receive an offer.

Below is a series of tips on how to thrive as a summer associate, formatted in terms of various issues that concern many summer associates. Regarding each of these issues, there are some things you should "Do" as well as some "don'ts" you should avoid. The book then analyzes in depth two particular perennial concerns of many summer associates - how to get an offer to join a niche group, and whether to begin as an associate in a litigation or transactional role.

1. Quality vs. Quantity in Work Assignments

<u>Do</u>:

... *your assignments perfectly in terms of optics, thoroughness, and process.* Take sufficient time to do a thorough job unless it is explicitly

---

[34] http://www.americanlawyer.com/id=1202780156373/Summer-Associate-Hiring-Was-Flat-in-2016.

communicated to you that there is a rushed time frame. (Of course, always ask about the time frame in advance so there are no misunderstandings.)

The same advice applies for all of your non-work related experiences at the firm - *what you do should be perfect*. If you're not sure if what you're going to say is stupid, just don't say it. What you do say should be smart.

But Don't:

... *worry about doing a lot of work*. There is plenty of time as an associate to work like crazy; summer associates are not expected to do so nor will there be a reward if you do. Your feedback at the end of the summer will be about the quality of your reviews, which will be based on the quality of your work product, not the number of hours you billed. Law firms generally don't even bill clients for summer associate hours and as long as you stay even remotely engaged in the work there will be no punishment for slow periods. To be clear, generally, you should avoid refusing work requested of you from the main department(s) you are interested in joining, but also think twice before reaching out if you don't have much work but your dormant transactions or litigation matters might reignite soon. A summer associate position isn't the type of job that you need to produce a certain amount; you should just not have a week at a time with nothing billed at all.

2. Who to Work For

Do:

... *work for several different cases or deal teams*. The assignment team responsible for divvying up assignments should do this for you, but occasionally without intervention you could get stuck on a single case or matter all summer or only a couple of matters. This is a very bad idea as it will appear strange why you received less reviews than other summer associates. If the one review you get is negative because of something you did the previous week, there will not be five other glowing reviews to outweigh it.

But Don't:

... worry about trying to work for rainmakers or to gain partner contact in general. Even as a junior associate and certainly as a summer associate, your main goal is fitting in and doing good work. You aren't expected to create relationships with attorneys as senior as partners. By all means, if you want to form relationships, do so, but there is no immediate need to do so - partners won't even remember your name when you rejoin the firm full-time and they may not remember it a week after you speak to them. Definitely make sure to not go over any associate's head as a summer associate.

3. What Departments to Work For

Do:

... try out various departments. If your firm has numerous departments, and you are even somewhat undecided about which department you are most interested in, a summer associate program is an ideal way to identify the practice area(s) in which you are interested and can succeed. For example, a summer associate program is the best, indeed the only, opportunity to try out that niche department or two that you want to know about.

In particular, I urge most people to take at least some assignments from both the litigation department and the corporate department, even if you are fairly certain you want to work full-time in one or the other or in a niche department. You may realize that you like the area you weren't initially interested in more. Potentially, even, the firm may have significantly less work in one or the other and if you haven't taken a single assignment in the busy department, it may be difficult for the firm to extend you an offer in the busy department.

But Don't:

... over-extend yourself in terms of the number of departments you are working for. If you are only taking work from a single department, it will be

rare for you to be working extremely hard during your summer, since the associates overseeing work distribution to summer associates in that department will make sure not to provide you too many assignments. On the other hand, if you are accepting work from five departments, you may found yourself in the uncomfortable position of refusing work because you are already busy with work provided by other departments, or worse, having multiple competing deadlines on your assignments from the different departments that you find difficult to meet.

4. What Type of Work to Do

<u>Do</u>:

... try to see the typical work that associates are doing in your areas of interest. Summer associates frequently receive assignments that are pre-packaged and have a clear start and end, such as doing research and writing a memorandum on a particular topic. However, associates and partners do a wide variety of work in which such clearly demarcated assignments hold vanishingly small importance. In making a decision on what department to enter, you should get a clear sense of whether you will have interest in the type of actual work that actual attorneys in the department - both junior and senior - actually perform. The smart firms will provide shadowing experiences for summer associates, but if yours doesn't, try to get invited or otherwise get involved in these experiences. At the very least, speak to associates and partners about their work, as what you learn may be eye-opening and influence your decision-making process.

<u>But Don't</u>:

... get caught up in trying to snag "cool" assignments and experiences to brag about to your fellow summer associates. This is another fetish of some hyper-competitive summer associates, and succeeding at this game will provide you absolutely nothing of practical value.

5. Summer Events

Do:

... *go to events and have a good time.* Summer events are a fundamental part of the program and thus even if they are technically "optional," you should go to any that you have the time and energy for, and even some that you don't. Certainly, if you have a unique situation with a deadline on an assignment and your firm has numerous events, missing one won't hurt you, but definitely don't be missed more than very occasionally and with good reason.

But Don't:

... *worry about actively "succeeding" at events.* Given how hyper-competitive lawyers are, and parallel to how some think they need to kill themselves on work during the summer, some think that they need to be the "#1 networker" among the summer class, and get to know every major partner and numerous associates. Take it easy. Again, at most firms, you don't need to stand out to get an offer, and if anything standing out can potentially hurt you.

Also, Don't:

... *do anything stupid.* This should be obvious to the vast majority of people, but do not drink more than one or two drinks, do not become overly comfortable with anyone at the firm, including summer associate program coordinators, who may seem to be the young party-hearty types, or your fellow summer associates, and certainly do not do anything unprofessional. There are, of course, numerous stories, most of them true, about summer associates who get no-offered, and potentially black-balled generally due to one stupid thing they did at a party. Such an attitude is justifiable: If you can't act professional for eight weeks, that's a problem.

6. Professionalism

Do:

... *take your experience seriously.* Summer associate programs are an amalgam of summer camp and ultra-important work that can be difficult to reconcile. Even if your firm provides the vast majority of summer associates with offers, they don't want it to seem automatic. If you ever imply that it is, they may find that offensive. Similarly, take it seriously even if you are intent on getting a job other than at a law firm. There is certainly nothing to lose from receiving an offer that you then politely decline. Even if you embark on a career in government, many government lawyers find themselves between jobs for various reasons. You may find it useful in such a position to cool your heels at a law firm job at a generous salary for a year or two - an option that may be available to you if you make a good impression and stay in touch.

Also Do:

... *dress well, perhaps, even better than you would as an associate.* While most firms have a business-casual policy and practice, you should keep to at least the conservative wing of that spectrum and perhaps even adopt business attire with suits or sport coats and ties and equivalent attire for women. It is the rare firm that such attire is out of place and it will affirm your professionalism.

But Don't:

... *feel the need to pretend you are an expert at anything.* You're not, and attempting to purport to be one may annoy associates and partners - the real experts. Be an eager mentee to attorneys at the firm.

Also, Don't:

... *say or do anything nasty to other summer associates.* Remember that word travels fast and even if it doesn't, these people will be your colleagues soon.

7. Getting into a Niche Department

One subset of summer associates interested in focused advice is the group looking for an offer to join a niche practice area. Some firms do not provide generalized offers to return to the firm but provide offers to start in particular departments. While at most of these firms the litigation and corporate transactional practice groups accept any summer associates who are allowed to return to the firm full-time, many smaller groups at firms are much more selective. Below, I offer background explanation regarding this dynamic and provide some strategic suggestions for successfully entering a niche practice group.

There are many reasons why smaller practice groups are selective. First and foremost, a department that is currently small, unless business is absolutely booming, cannot grow headcount quickly or there may not be enough work to go around. Departments such as entertainment simply don't usually have all that much work and there is simply not a need for many, if any, new associates. In addition, many small departments, such as T&E, ERISA and tax in some firms, and real estate in others, serve as service departments to other departments at the firm and do not bring in clients, and as a result have less influence to be able to bring in new associates. Finally, some such departments, such as bankruptcy or real estate, are cyclical and thus even if work is plentiful now, the department does not want to overhire due to concerns work may slow down in the future, which would leave staff with little to do.

The first strategy in obtaining an offer to join a small group is to **broadcast your interest in a clear but not needy way.** If you want to get an offer from a particular department, you need to make it clear that you are interested in working in that department and would prefer an offer in that department to a generalized offer. This seems obvious but some people are shy or are otherwise reticent about making their desires clear. Perhaps, this is because they remain nervous about receiving an offer of any kind.

However, you should manage your message by being clear that you are not dead-set on that particular practice area and would welcome any opportunity to return to the firm. Some firms may view those who are gunning too aggressively for a particular department as individuals who may not be happy or perform well in another department, or generally as individuals who may not recognize the great opportunity presented by any offer to return to the firm.

Next, you should **put the above message into practice in approaching work assignments**. You should approach the attorneys in the niche department for work assignments; ideally, you should work for at least a few of the department's attorneys so they can get to know you and your work. However, again, don't go overboard - there's no need to complete numerous assignments or devote the majority of your summer work to the department. If you complete several assignments with aplomb, that will sufficiently indicate that you perform quality work and completing another three will not change that assessment.

You should **approach other aspects of the summer program in a similar manner**. Be sure to go to the events put on by the department in which you are interested, and speak with many of the department's members. Be clear about your interest but don't be overbearing about it, as there is an inherent psychological desire to squash such over-excitement.

Ultimately, you need to **manage your emotions and expectations**. The firm generally, including the department you are interested in, is a business, and if there is not a business case to adding new associates to the department, the firm will not do so. Even if there is, you may simply be passed over for another summer associate, as the reality is that for such positions you are in a zero sum game with other summer associates.

Ultimately, it is actually true that receiving any offer to return to the firm is a great opportunity, with numerous financial and career benefits, which is why you joined the summer program in the first place. Appreciate your success realistically, even if you didn't get exactly what you wanted.

8. Litigation vs. Corporate

One final question facing many summer associates is whether to begin practice in a litigation practice or in a transactional role. In fact, this is probably the most important decision for a young attorney to make, more important than which firm to pick or which law school to go to.

These two practice areas are fundamentally different and the best fit for you may depend on your psychological makeup. Transactional practice, of any kind, looks to complete deals and realize successful outcomes for clients, and attracts personalities that like to be helpful and accomplish tasks. It may, on the other hand, repel those who prefer big ideas to hours of highly detail-oriented work and talking rather than doing. To be sure, smooth-talking clients and counterparties is an asset and perhaps a requirement for a certain level of success in transactional practice as well, and litigation practice has its own crushing burden of detail-oriented work. However, generally transactional practice is more detail-oriented than litigation practice.

Litigation practice, on the other hand, results from problems arising from failed or problematic transactions or relationships. It may attract those who are analytical, opinionated and argumentative. Further, while the hot-headed litigator is largely a silly stereotype, and a wide variety of personalities can succeed in the field, it certainly is true that litigation is ultimately about disputes and you should be comfortable getting up in a courtroom, deposition or in meetings with governmental representatives and confidently and aggressively pursuing your client's case and degrading the other side's. It is well-known that junior litigators rarely receive such opportunities, but you should be confident in your ability to succeed in such environments when the time comes.

All else being equal, purely economic considerations generally weigh in favor of transactional practice, based on the law of supply and demand. In terms of supply, there is a larger supply of litigators than transactional attorneys for several reasons. Law students are drawn to litigation practice given the interest they may have had in the subject before or during law school, the basic familiarity they may have with the practice, and simply finding the practice area interesting. In addition, litigation is practiced by law firms across the prestige spectrum, including solo practitioners, while transactional practice, especially certain niches, is more confined to larger and more prestigious firms.

With regard to demand, there is generally more demand for transactional attorneys. Litigation is the practice area offering jobs most skewed to private practice in a law firm, as while there are an increasing number of corporations looking to hire in-house attorneys to oversee litigation matters, there are still far fewer in-house litigation jobs than transactional or advisory jobs. While essentially all large law firms have robust litigation practices, at many firms it is a relatively stable practice that does not serve as an engine of growth for the law firm's business, and in some cases litigation practice largely services the clients generated by the firm's corporate practice (although to be fair at other firms it is the opposite or at the very least both the corporate and litigation practice generate their own clients). This means that firms don't feel the need to promote a lot of partners in litigation, given that it is not a profit engine and litigation associates have less options than transactional associates.

Given the combination of numerous large firm lawyers practicing within the area, with the lack of strategic importance of these practices to firms, plus the lack of in-house opportunities, plus the availability of many lawyers working as litigators at small and mid-size law firms, plus the general ability of litigators to generalize rather than specialize in a particular niche within litigation, mid-level transactional attorneys will generally have more opportunities available to them than their litigator counterparts with equivalent pedigree. To be fair, you should not enter any practice that you hate, nor likely will you succeed in such work. Moreover, transactional attorneys may find themselves unemployed with few prospects in the event that the economy goes into a severe recession, as occurred to many attorneys during the Great Recession in 2008-2009. And for those interested in governmental or public service, litigation is clearly the better choice.

However, if you are simply interested in maximizing your mid-career earnings, transactional practice is definitely a better bet.

Chapter 14: Surviving and ~~Thriving~~ Surviving in the Lions' Den: Making it as an Associate

Working at a law firm will be an intense experience. This book is not going to change that. A law firm will stretch your emotional strength, physical endurance, political savvy, intellectual capability, and creativity, to their respective limits. You cannot control that, nor can you control how individuals at a law firm treat you or various other variables related to your experience there.

But what you can control is how you conduct yourself, approach the work and the people at a law firm, and look out for your interests. Associates of course have a wide range of experiences at law firms, and working with what you can change will have an impact on your experience, whether it lasts six months or 45 years, and make that experience more positive.

The below provides a variety of tips in approaching this unique experience. It is divided into five sections outlining approaches to (a) excelling at the legal work provided to you; (b) adapting to firm politics and "playing the game"; (c) keeping the business objectives of the law firm in mind; (d) how to approach the ultimate goal of a law firm - excellent client service; and (e) "looking out for number one" and making sure that you protect your own well-being.

A. The Work

1. *Always learn.*

In the course of your work at a law firm, you will be provided with a wide variety of tasks. Some will be boring, others will be difficult, still others will suck your very lifeblood out of you. Some tasks may be thrilling. Whatever your interest in a task or its seeming importance or lack thereof to the client or the legal matter, you should learn something from everything you do. If you are doing document review or due diligence, pay attention to the content and context of the documents you review to learn about the client and the business processes and industry involved. If you have been given a small part in a large matter, try to understand the larger context and the rest of the facts of the litigation or the other parts of the deal whenever possible. When reviewing contracts or cases, try to digest more than the specific language or point you are seeking and use such seemingly lowly tasks to become an expert about the topics and context involved. The time you spend on work is a fixed cost - you can't eliminate the drudgery by not paying attention. What you can do to make your time better spent is to gain as much as you can from every experience.

2. *Seek out work.*

You should seek out work, rather than simply perform the work that is provided you. How matters and tasks are assigned to junior associates is a byzantine, opaque, largely irrational process at almost every firm. Much of the time, it's a crapshoot. While I'm not doubting that you are a genius, highly attractive and charming, you should not assume that everyone has the same opinion or that those aspects of you will result in you receiving the work that you want. Proactive associates distinguish themselves and, it should be obvious, will be more likely to receive whatever assignment is being provided than a comparably qualified but mute associate. To be sure, if an associate is overbearing, annoying, or simply perceived as overly aggressive, such tactics can backfire, but the benefits from pursuing work far outweigh the potential negatives. This advice is certainly true in those firms which employ a "free market" system, where there is no central assignment system and associates seeking and partners providing must match themselves, but applies even in firms where there is such a system. If a partner says that they want to work with associate X, the person in charge of the assignment system, who frequently is not even a practicing attorney, will certainly never object.

While being proactive is a good idea generally, it is in particular useful to accomplish two specific goals. The first is to keep "busy[35]" when work is light. When there is not that much work to go around, some associates will have to get picked over others. Partners and senior associates will appreciate knowing that you are interested in working with them, no matter how self-serving such statements may seem to you, and they will be more likely, all else being equal, to pick you over another associate that remains in the background.

The second is to get staffed on matters involving particular legal issues, clients or industries in which you are interested. Get to know the people who work on such matters, and sign up for whatever comes down the pike, no matter how low-level or inconvenient in terms of scheduling the initial work may seem. Some associates complain after a few years at a law firm that they only received low-level work, or did not receive work in their area of interest. Many of these associates do not have any right to complain, because they did little to nothing affirmatively to land the type of work they wanted.

3. *Seek out good work.*

Relatedly, not all work, and not all legal matters, are created equal. Working on high-profile matters - deals or cases involving a very large amount of money, prominent parties, and/or that are featured in the news - will impress people both inside and outside the firm more than work on lower-profile matters. Frequently, simply being a team member on such a case is beneficial to one's standing in a firm. Similarly, working on tasks that are considered more important (whether or not they are in reality more difficult

---

[35] The word "busy" is the actual word law firms use to describe how hard associates should work, and in turn how everyone at law firms describe what they are up to. They should "keep busy." "How are you? Busy." A term equal parts ridiculous in its reduction of high-profile high-complexity legal matters to the equivalent of mindless sausage making, and telling in its exclusive focus on the needs of the law firm without any regard to the actual needs of its clients, who are paying the law firm for its associates' "keeping busy" at their expense.

or not) and therefore more likely to be assigned to someone more senior will be more impressive than those that are lower in importance.

Without being overly pushy, you should make it a priority to get high-profile work and high-level tasks. At a law firm, these two criteria are frequently inverse - the more high-profile the matter, the less likely you are to receive high-level work, and vice versa. Given the inverse relationship, you should look to get staffed on a mix of high-profile and low-profile matters, to get the benefits of working on high-profile matters that accrues regardless of what you actually do, and the substantive experience of the high-level tasks that are easier to gain on low-profile matters. If you can bag high-level experience on a high-profile case, that will reflect quite well on you inside the firm assuming you don't screw the work up, and will certainly reflect well on a resume or in an interview.

One caveat to this point is to avoid being overly eager to perform complicated tasks unless you are quite confident that you have the skills to execute flawlessly. Many associates flock to tasks involving "greater responsibility" without realizing that working on tasks that are more important also means that screwing up on those tasks is a bigger deal. If someone entrusts you with something important and you screw it up, they might never trust you again, and your new reputation as a screw-up might also ricochet throughout the firm, permanently dooming your associateship. The caveat to this caveat is that sometimes, counterintuitively, higher-level responsibilities for which one can prepare and devote extended amounts of time present less danger of looking bad than responsibilities that are less intellectual and relatively quick and so are considered lower-level but for which perfect execution remains critical.

Countervailingly, there are types of work to studiously avoid to the extent possible. One such category is work that is administrative in nature and not intellectual, and thus successfully completing such tasks will not impress anyone, while making a mistake will be disastrous for the deal or case. You will certainly need to complete some such work, but try to avoid such work to the extent your efforts will not make you appear lazy. You can do this through, e.g., volunteering for assignments other than these when multiple choices are available.

A second type of work to avoid is work on a matter that is considered extremely commoditized. Sometimes clients are willing to pay higher billing rates for work that a smaller law firm could do for lower rates, and /or some law firms will take a large discount on some work if they have excess capacity and /or want to develop a relationship of any kind with a particular client. There is nothing wrong with doing some work of this kind, but avoid - at all costs - having this work take over a large part of your practice. No one will be impressed, either inside or outside the law firm.

Finally, avoid working for senior attorneys who are simply nasty. Many attorneys are difficult to work with but ultimately appreciate a job well done and working with such people can be richly rewarding, in some instances more rewarding than working with the purported "nice guys." Others, however, are simply nasty, and seem to rejoice over finding errors, real or imaginary, in work performed while unable to have a concomitant appreciation for outstanding work. Avoid such people at all costs; at the end of the day, if you don't work for them, they can't submit performance reviews for you.

4. *Work hard.*

One would think that working hard is an involuntary, fundamental part of working at a law firm. Sometimes that is the case, but it is still good advice for many associates to make sure to work hard. The harder you work - adding more matters, more tasks, more clients, more pro bono, more everything - the more you will know, the more your legal skills will improve, and the more people, both inside and outside the law firm, you will get exposed to and hopefully impress. Ultimately, there is a reason that associates keep coming back to large law firms that churn through associates by making them bill thousands of hours per year - because the associates coming out the other side have attained a wealth of information, knowledge, know-how and know-who at least in part due to all of that backbreaking churning they went through.

There will be various excuses to work less hard at a law firm - including that the individual matters you are staffed on, the partners you working with, or your niche simply have less work available at the time. Working hard even when you fall into such circumstances will buoy your career in myriad ways. Looking for more work when work is slow may also help you to avoid getting pigeon-holed working on all-consuming matters or with someone you don't get along with, although of course doing so carries with it the potential to get slammed from all sides at once. Working with more people will give you greater name recognition within the firm and give you at least a basic familiarity with other types of legal matters.

5. *Process, not results, matter.*

Sometimes associates can get caught up in the importance of the legal matter to the client and overstep their role based on a view that the client and the senior members of the team are desperately looking to accomplish a particular end goal and will tolerate breaks to protocol to get there. Based on this view, associates will sometimes become overly alarmed about particular problems or overly excited about potential solutions they have thought of.

Don't flatter yourself. The legal matters involved are highly complex and your particular problem or issue may be overshadowed by far larger concerns and goals of the client. For example, an issue that would be relevant if the case is brought to trial or a motion actually ruled on may be largely irrelevant if settlement is the ultimate goal, and an issue in due diligence may be covered by standard representations and warranties. Issues that appear novel and knotty to you as a relatively inexperienced lawyer may likewise be routine to those more experienced.

Also, don't be so naïve. There is an intertwining of interest between the senior lawyers' duties to the client and their duties to themselves. Senior lawyers want to control, either directly or through trusted lieutenants, the matters they are involved in, and want the work performed on those matters to reflect well on them and not on others. To the extent there is competition for the good graces of a client, or of a rainmaker partner, lawyers will at times work to ensure they stay in those good graces even if such efforts may potentially come in partial conflict with the interests of the client in having every rock equally uncovered. Frequently, it is ambiguous what the "best result" even is, with disappointments in deal terms or litigation matters that can be chalked up to unavoidable circumstances instead of failures by legal counsel.

Indeed, such human dynamics are not exclusively the domain of law firms; in-house lawyers at clients will have political situations that are equally, if not more, complex. In-house lawyers carefully guide legal matters to reflect most positively on their own efforts just as much as to ensure the "best" result for the corporation. Other than ensuring that the explicit wishes of senior management are fulfilled, in-house counsel also gives itself a significant amount of wiggle room, such as through reserving more for a litigation than what they actually estimate as the expected result in order to ultimately achieve results that are better than the reserve initially made.

6. *Results also matter.*

All that being said, it is still definitely better to close a big deal, achieve a client's objectives, and win cases. If you are still standing on a case or deal team when that happens, that will generally enhance your standing at the law firm, especially if it is a team for which you serve as a senior associate. Others both inside and outside the firm will look more favorably at such objective results than more ambiguous results from other teams even if the more ambiguous results required more effort and ingenuity.

B. Politics / "The Game"

1. *First impressions count.*

Your supervisors at law firms will frequently be prone to quick and lasting judgments about new associates and associates with whom they work for the first time. This may because attorneys are naturally judgmental, or simply because partners and other senior attorneys will work with numerous associates that come and go, given the high-attrition model at many law firms. This reality is both a problem and an opportunity; those who stumble initially may be relegated to second-tier matters and areas of responsibilities without the opportunity to develop over time, while those who emerge strong out of the blocks will have an advantage and may quickly be given leadership opportunities at a firm. If you have obtained good skills in these areas prior to beginning work as a lawyer, you may have received a lasting advantage over those who have not.

2. *Don't care too much.*

The elite financial, legal and business world prefers personalities that are supremely confident but not emotional or overly excited. While you may be very excited by the matters you are working on by your ideas in particular, do your best to remain cool and collected at all times. Of course, this becomes more challenging after you log those multiple all-nighters, but remaining chill comes with a reward - many law firm leaders will tell you that are drawn to those associates that can remain unflappable even under such significant stress.

3. *Smart is as smart does.*

One common misconception of succeeding in a law firm is that those that are more "objectively" the "better lawyers" - with the best arguments, the most creative ideas, the hardest work ethics - will rise to the top. In reality, succeeding at a law firm is just as much about showmanship and sounding smart than any objective measure. In a large law firm, just like in many work environments, your ability to appear smart - sound smart, look smart, and act smart - is just as important as being smart. This is not a completely irrational stance by law firms. Partners may view those that appear confident, tough while deferential when appropriate, sophisticated and crafty in internal meetings as also more likely to get ahead in a high-stakes corporate negotiation or trial. As a result, you choosing style over substance at a junior level may be a safer choice.

4. *Agree.*

Junior associates should generally look to be strongly deferential and agreeable with their superiors. There is a natural human tendency to like people who like you and agree with your ideas. Lawyers in particular can be quite insecure, perhaps in part due to personality and in part due to the harsh treatment that the lawyers may have in the past or currently receive from clients or superiors.

Erring on the side of deference over challenge is thus always a safe bet. That's not to say that you should never venture new ideas, but you should look to place them strategically in situations where the senior lawyers have broadcast that they are open to them. There's also not a lot to lose from not pushing you own ideas. Junior lawyers are not really expected to have creative substantive ideas. Indeed, more senior attorneys, who view themselves as possessing knowledge and insight only possibly conferred via experience, may view defensively a junior associate frequently or aggressively expressing such ideas.

5. *This too shall pass.*

At a law firm, you are certain to go through ups and downs - in terms of how much you are working, your interest in what you are doing, your relationship with your co-workers and supervisors, and a variety of other ways. Chill out. Too many associates get caught up in the day to day politics and turbulence without appreciating that working at a law firm is a growth engine for you. Whatever is bothering you will likely reverse itself in a couple of days. Too busy? Your deal might collapse or your case might settle tomorrow. Not doing anything? Enjoy it while it lasts! Similar sentiments apply to difficulties in working with particular people or on particular issues or tasks - work through it and it will likely improve soon. If you are really bothered, go to therapy regularly - and don't think for a minute you're weird or atypical, as therapists build entire careers counseling big firm lawyers.

6. *Don't fret or crow over your drift through the law firm "class structure."*

Most associates will have some experiences at a law firm that make them feel important and other experiences that make them feel degraded. On some teams or matters, you may occupy a leading role, taking on more responsibility than your fellow associates. Enjoy it while it lasts, but do not allow yourself to get arrogant and make mistakes, get lulled into complacency, or treat others badly. On others, you may be stuck doing routine work or even taking orders from an associate from your own class year or even, in some situations, someone junior to yourself. Swallow your pride and move on, and do not let this short-term blip cause you to convince yourself that it reflects something more permanent or react in a way that will indeed damage your standing at the firm. Law firms are not kindergartens, and there will be ebbs and flows in how you are treated - buck up.

7. *Consider the political landscape before getting ahead.*

In looking to gain more substantive experience or a strong relationship with a partner or other senior lawyer, junior associates may find themselves in situations where they run the risk of stepping on the toes of other senior lawyers. Consider the consequences of such actions carefully. It may be that the responsibility enjoyed will end quickly, and the partner you thought you were ingratiating yourself towards never calls you again, but the anger and hurt feelings remain and potentially hurt you in future dealings with the people involved.

There's no one answer to such issues. Some associates do indeed shortcut their way to enhanced relationships and significant responsibility, while others crash and burn. Rather, in each situation you have to carefully gauge the landscape and weigh the benefits against the risks. Like in other human situations, consider cues carefully and be honest with yourself:

Has the partner or senior lawyer you believe you are developing a relationship with reached out to you, or is all of the outreach coming from you to him or her?

Has the partner really given you signals that they will send you a lot of work in the future, or are they simply grateful for the extra help?

Have they broadcast signals to others on the team that they view you as important to signal to the other team members to in turn treat you with deference, or have they continued to treat you like any other associate in public?

These are the types of questions you should be asking yourself before taking relationship risks.

C. The Business

1. *Look out for number one, because no one else is.*

So many associates do not fully appreciate some very simple truths, each of which seemingly should go without saying. Repeat after me: A law firm is a business that exclusively looks out for its own interests - not yours. Partners at law firms look out for their own interests, not yours. Senior associates are looking out for their own interests, not yours. The head of associate development is looking out for his or her own interests and not yours.

For some reason, perhaps due to the theoretical nature of much of law school studies, the public-service interests of many young lawyers, the educational institution-like structure of organizing associates by class year, or the simple lack of time they have due to the enormity of their responsibilities, junior associates frequently entrust the responsibilities for their personal and career development to their employer law firms. Associates become passive, and simply take the work provided to them, rather than developing goals and critically examining, on a regular basis, their progress towards those goals.

Associates have to actively ensure that they come out better due to their experience at a law firm and not simply assume that that will be the case. If you want to ensure you have exit options, it is your responsibility to build your resume and reputation - not your law firm's. If you want particular type of work or want to work with particular people, it is your responsibility to seek that out - not a partner's. If you want to be acknowledged for good work you have performed, or avoid blame for mistakes that were not your fault, it is your responsibility to ensure that happens - not a senior associate's. Got it?

2. Get out more.

It is easy, given the amount of work foisted upon them, for associates to only speak to other attorneys on the teams they work on, and perhaps associates in their class year that they knew from the summer associate program. Resist this urge and get out more. Get to know associates and partners in other practice groups, on both the litigation and corporate side, and other attorneys in your practice group. Go to firm events, practice group lunches and other get-togethers.

There are numerous benefits to doing so. First, many, many legal matters require attorneys from more than one practice group, and an easy way to be bill hours and get more exposure to clients is to be referred a matter by an attorney in another department. Even if you don't get credit for the origination, consulting for other departments is a convenient way to bill hours that can also expand your knowledge base. Moreover, having contacts in other departments also provides you a trusted source for advice about areas of law regarding which you are unfamiliar; sometimes you may actually bring them into a matter and in other cases you may simply be seeking a "gut check," but either way it can be a lifesaver. Finally, similar to what this book discussed with regard to law school, working at a large law firm is an incredible networking opportunity, with close exposure to lots of highly credentialed attorneys that can provide you jobs and business in the future. Take advantage while you can.

In addition, make sure to continue networking outside of your law firm. Becoming active in your local bar association, or otherwise participating in a pro bono organization, or even taking the time to hang out with your friends from law school are all examples of ways that can help you in a variety of ways. Introducing yourself to senior attorneys outside of your law firm can lead to exit options, and networking with attorneys at your level allows you to share war stories in a way that you may feel unsafe doing inside your law firm, and to gain insight into practice and politics from others who identify with your experiences.

3. *You're not a pigeon; don't get pigeon-holed.*

Sophisticated lawyers have never been general practitioners. At large law firms, attorneys also are usually not general transactional or general litigation lawyers, but focus on a particular practice area or focus area within one of those two categories. And, for a couple of decades now, large law firms have pushed their attorneys to increasing levels of sub-specialization. The law firms do it because clients demand experts and the law firms can demand higher billing rates for highly specialized attorneys.

However, this trend presents multiple dangers for the attorneys involved. An attorney with a more focused practice has a smaller universe of exit options than an attorney with a broader practice. Moreover, although specialization may give the associate better chances of landing exit options for positions seeking attorneys within the sub-niche, if the market has little demand for the niche or if it comes to view the niche as commoditized, the attorney's skills can become irrelevant.

There are two ways for a new attorney to mitigate these concerns. First, all else being equal, look to join a law firm that provides junior associates with as general experience in litigation or transactional practice as possible. The ideal, in this sense, is Sullivan & Cromwell, where the transactional practice is not sub-divided into sub-groups. Unfortunately, that system is quite rare, and made possible largely because that firm's outstanding reputation attracts clients to it regardless of the specialization of its attorneys.

However, many other firms do provide attorneys in the first or second year of practice with exposure to multiple practice areas within transactional or litigation practice - try to get a job with those firms if at all possible. It is monumentally difficult for an attorney as inexperienced as a summer associate to make long-term decisions about a career, beyond whether to focus on transactional or litigation practice. Working at a firm where new attorneys gain exposure to multiple areas can provide the attorneys with helpfully broad exposure as well as allow them to make mid-course corrections to their initial plan.

The second way to implement this point is to make sure that you don't get overly sucked into the workflow of one particular partner or sub-group. Some attorneys get involved in a legal matter involving a sub-niche, and the partner(s) overseeing the sub-niche take(s) a liking to the attorney. Several years later, the attorney may find himself or herself looking to leave the firm, voluntarily or not, with, given the limited nature of the attorney's experience, few options outside of the sub-niche. For various reasons that sub-niche may have very few to no exit options available for that attorney.

This advice applies to both deal lawyers and litigation attorneys, but may be more important for litigators to observe. In some cases, litigation associates may focus on a single matter for years at a time, finding themselves several years later with few to no options given their lack of relevant experience outside of the unique idiosyncrasies of that case. Again, guarding yourself in this way is exclusively your responsibility, not the responsibility of your firm or the partners involved.

D. The Clients

1. *Learn about your clients.*

Above, I urged you to always try to learn from everything you do. You should in particular try to learn as much as possible about your clients - their business model, their business practices, their industry, their fears and their hopes. This can help you communicate better with them, as they will be more receptive to what you say if you phrase it in their language. It can help you win business, as clients are drawn to lawyers that they view as general advisors more than pure legal technocrats. And it can get you jobs, as clients want in-house lawyers who work seamlessly as part of their business and understand it well.

2. *Be an expert.*

Clients are under the impression that outside lawyers are experts in the fields they practice. That's why they pay them such gigantic rates. If you want to gain the respect of clients and potentially win business, you cannot just counsel clients as to the specific issues they are dealing with. You need to project that you are an expert who is superior to others in your field and a trusted ally that has everything under control. If you betray either of those perceptions, you will have frustrated clients that you need to explain yourself to; if you betray both, even if the problem concerns something that has little to no practical import to the client, you're gone.

3. *Talk about other stuff.*

Clients are also people, and, like everyone else, like lawyers with whom they are comfortable and enjoy being around. One good way to foster that connection, even if you are not naturally charismatic, is to engage the client in conversation regarding topics other than your assignment. In a manner that is appropriate for the amount of time you have worked with the client, you can ask about the client's business or simply about the client's life. You can do this in person over drinks, food or at an event, but even outside of such literal "client development" activities, which clients know law firms organize simply to derive more business from their organization, you should look to appropriately converse with clients over the phone after discussing the legal matters at hand. Above all, portray yourself as someone supportive of the client within his or her organization and generally; many in-house attorneys find themselves in political situations that are just as knotty as large law firms, and support from a sophisticated outsider can go a long way.

4. *Be responsive.*

Clients greatly appreciate responsiveness. No one cares that outside lawyers are incredibly busy, and many clients find it incredibly offensive when attorneys take days to respond to them. Make it a priority to get back to every client on the day they reach out to you, and preferably as soon as possible.

E. You

1. *Treat yourself like the fancy-pants you are - not the rag you sometimes feel like.*

As this book has hopefully beaten into your head, working at a law firm is tough - not just in terms of lifestyle, but psychologically and emotionally as well. You may view many of the tasks you perform as degrading; other attorneys may treat you poorly, even at times arguably abuse you; clients are guaranteed to run you ragged. Continued experiences in this vein may alter your view of yourself. While prior to working at a law firm you may have felt highly accomplished, perhaps even, fairly or not, on the highest rungs of society, you may now feel like an overeducated failure with little to offer the world.

Don't let that happen. You are a success and can be extraordinarily successful no matter what happens at your law firm. As noted above, every attorney at a law firm goes through periods where they are treated as "second-class" and every attorney performs some low-level tasks as part of their career. If you have become an attorney at all, that is already an accomplishment beyond the dreams of many Americans. Most non-lawyers, even high-powered business people, don't quite understand the differences between different law firms, so any experience at a law firm, even if it is not an elite one, will benefit you greatly in a wide variety of fields. If you went to an elite school and/or attained a job with a solid law firm, those are accomplishments that will highly impress many throughout your career regardless of how well you did in school or how short your stay at the firm is. If you gain some high-profile experience at the law firm, or are even earning high salaries, you have vaulted to a rarefied level that in turn greatly increases the chances of attaining high-powered and lucrative jobs in the future, again regardless of what happens at the law firm.

Carry yourself at the law firm like the high-powered guy or gal you are. Not only will this improve your mood, it will help your performance and help you navigate politics better.

2. *Enjoy the perks.*

Working at a law firm, especially a large law firm, carries with it numerous perks that associates may not fully appreciate until they leave the firm and do not have them. Many law firms will provide a car service and dinner to associates who work late. Many provide excellent benefits, including providing and encouraging attorneys to take extended paid and gender-neutral family leave. The salaries are frequently high and increase automatically with increased seniority. Attorneys are provided extensive support services, including paralegals, secretarial support, and whole departments that handle reproduction, document editing, court filings, and other services.

If and when you leave the law firm, these perks may vanish. You may work late for a big corporation or the government but have to take late-night buses instead of a comfy car. You may have to make tough decisions about how soon to return after a birth or other family event. You may have reduced salaries with no window into when increases will happen. You may have to do all your own administrative work yourself. Enjoy it while it lasts.

3. *Minimize the impact on your family or friends.*

The taxing nature of law firm or corporate life ruins many marriages, friendships, and familial relationships. Law firms take people away, in sum and substance, from their families and acquaintances for days, months, and years at a time. Lawyers can internalize the politics and emotionally taxing nature of legal practice and take such emotions out on their loved ones.

Do you have a goal of gaining or maintaining strong relationships with a significant other, spouse, family member, child, or friend? If you work at a law firm, you have to plan carefully before you start working and focus every day when you are working about how to accomplish that goal.

The first issue to consider in this vein is time. You will have much less time while working at a law firm than you did previously. You need to plan and set expectations - there is no way you can work at a major law firm for even a short time if you will be expected to be home every day by 7 p.m. or always make evening or weekend plans. Another example - you will likely need to increase your spending on outside housekeeping to make up for the loss of any such work you may have previously done.

While previously you may have had plenty of time to spend together, now you need to aggressively seek alternative ways to strengthen relationships, which will wither and die if you spend no time together. Generally, you should look to take advantage of time you do not need to spend in the office. Many law firms do not have any expectation that associates work in the office at night except when a litigation or deal is at a critical stage. Some find it difficult to work efficiently at home, but if you are at all able to do so, it will greatly improve your home relationships if you can leave the office, have dinner or otherwise spend some time with those close to you, and then continue working from home.

There are strategies you can employ to maintain relationships even during the times when you are hardest hit. Talk during the work day - if you only have a few minutes, make them quality minutes by focusing on the call rather than simply replying with short responses while continuing to look at your computer screen or a document. Having lunch together if your spouse works or lives nearby is also a great option. Another option is to make sure to spend at least a few minutes at home together even if it is very late at night. Finally, when you have to work on the weekends, which may be every weekend during some periods, try to work from home or share some time together each day.

You should try your utmost to maintain relationships with your family and friends as well. Work comes first, but rare is the firm that you cannot get away from for occasional dinners with friends or outing on occasional weekends. Seize opportunities when they arise - again, it's not that you can't have an outside life while working at a law firm, you just need to be more vigilant and aggressive about it. You will certainly need to cancel at times, but avoid getting so caught up with the universe of your law firm that you lose your appreciation for what your friends and family have done for you. Your law firm universe could and will likely end at some point, and at that point you will be dearly disappointed if your relationships with others have degraded or disappeared.

3. *Take care of yourself.*

Make sure to maintain your wellbeing while working. Too many lawyers become overweight and physically unfit while at a law firm, due to the long hours, frequent eating out, travel, and stress that such jobs entail.

There are three specific ways you should go about doing this. First, work out regularly. Again, like with maintaining outside relationships, this is possible, it just may be extremely late at night or in abbreviated spurts, rather than the long workouts you may have engaged in prior to working. Second, eat healthy. Even if you are ordering from take out every night, take steps such as replacing a side dish with a salad and maintaining proper portions. In addition, avoid frequent snacking during the day, unless it involves fruits and vegetables. And, while this may sound ridiculous, make sure to always keep yourself clean and groomed, and buy yourself nice clothes. No matter how harried partners and other senior attorneys will make you, they will still expect you to look your best as the price of admission for the high-powered job you have attained.